THE COMPLETE ILLUSTRATED BOOK O
NAPKINS AND
NAPKIN FOLDIN

THE COMPLETE ILLUSTRATED BOOK OF
NAPKINS AND
NAPKIN FOLDING

HOW TO CREATE SIMPLE AND ELEGANT DISPLAYS FOR EVERY OCCASION,
WITH 150 IDEAS FOR FOLDING, MAKING, DECORATING AND EMBELLISHING

1100 BEAUTIFUL PHOTOGRAPHS SHOW YOU HOW – WITH PROFESSIONAL TIPS
AND INSPIRATIONAL IDEAS FOR PLACE SETTINGS AND TABLE DECORATIONS

Rick Beech

southwater

Contents

Introduction

Whether you are preparing a formal feast or a simple lunch, the table sets the scene for the meal, and a beautifully and elegantly laid table creates a sense of anticipation among your guests, who can look forward to a special time together. Every table setting combines items that you use repeatedly, such as plates and glasses, with more transient elements such as flowers that give each meal a unique atmosphere. As you plan your design you'll want to take lots of things into account – the time of day, the formality of the meal, the décor of the room, and even the food you will be serving, and it's the decorative details that play a huge role in making your table look beautiful and right.

While we would all love the opportunity to start from scratch with the ideal tableware for each occasion, this is obviously not viable. In reality, few of us have the cupboard space, let alone the money, to acquire endless sets of china and glass to cater perfectly for every entertaining event. The best solution is to concentrate on the details.

You really can create completely different looks and moods simply by changing the accessories. A table dressed for dinner in crisp white linen and your best china, then accessorized with sparkling cut glass, flickering candles and inventively folded napkins, immediately sets a formal mood for a special occasion, perhaps an important celebration. For a different kind of meal you might simply replace starched white napkins with extrovert lime green ones, folded at each place or tucked into brightly coloured napkin rings, and guests will immediately anticipate an altogether more informal and relaxed affair.

The key is to invest in classic pieces of china, glass and cutlery that you know you will continue to enjoy using for years to come. These pieces will be the basic ingredients for your table settings, and you can dress them up or down to create the right ambience for each occasion. Candles and flowers, with their natural seasonal variety, have always been a quick way to make a change, but of all the other elements of table setting the easiest and most cost effective to change or adapt are the linens.

You can't go wrong by investing in exquisite white or cream dinner napkins in linen or cotton damask. Really good quality table linens last a lifetime – or more, as they can be handed down from one generation to the next. Freshly laundered, they always look wonderful, and years of hot washing and starching give linens and heavy cottons an appearance and feel that goes

Left Royal blue napkins and gold tableware are a perfect combination for a formal outdoor occasion. When used together these colours suggest formality and luxury.

Above *A rosebud is both a simple and extravagant way to add a finishing touch to a table setting. Held in place with a delicate ribbon, this final flourish adds to the occasion. Team with old-fashioned plates and good quality neutral fabric napkins.*

Right *Red is the perfect colour for a festive table setting. Co-ordinating crackers decorated with gold complements the china plate perfectly.*

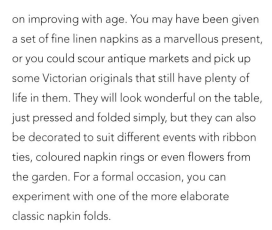

on improving with age. You may have been given a set of fine linen napkins as a marvellous present, or you could scour antique markets and pick up some Victorian originals that still have plenty of life in them. They will look wonderful on the table, just pressed and folded simply, but they can also be decorated to suit different events with ribbon ties, coloured napkin rings or even flowers from the garden. For a formal occasion, you can experiment with one of the more elaborate classic napkin folds.

Alternatively, and there is no reason why you should not do both for ultimate flexibility, you can pick up a few sets of napkins in contemporary colours and designs from fashionable interiors stores. For less than the cost of a vase of flowers

you can buy a set of napkins that will instantly change the look of your table. Added to your classic tableware they will give your table settings a whole new slant. You can transform the look of the table further by changing the way you fold the napkins or by adding some simple decoration.

Packed into this book you'll find a host of creative ways to use napkins in a wide range of settings and for every occasion, from weddings to picnics. You can discover novel ways to fold, knot, wrap, embroider and decorate them, as well as making original napkin rings out of all kinds of materials, from beaded wire to safety pins. These inspirational ideas, beautifully presented, will transform the way you think about napkins and add a fresh dimension to all your meals.

Napkins through history

There's something so deeply satisfying about the look and feel of crisp, freshly laundered white linen that it has endured internationally as the most popular table covering for hundreds of years. Shaking a clean white tablecloth and letting it float down over the table is almost a ritual in many households; it's the formal beginning of every feast, whether it is a small family meal or a state banquet.

The individual element of table linen is the napkin. One is provided for each diner, to protect their clothes from spills and stains, to protect their hands when holding hot dishes and plates, and to dab lips and greasy fingertips. In fact, these are all functions for which the tablecloth itself was once used, and the word "napkin" comes directly from nappe, the French word for a tablecloth.

Saving the tablecloth

Napkins were unheard of in Europe until the Middle Ages, by which time there was clearly a desperate need for them. Cutlery was not widely used and people ate mostly with their hands,

which they then wiped clean on a part of the tablecloth. As each part of the meal was finished a messy debris of food built up and the cloth had to be changed, a rather disruptive procedure that held up the progress of the meal and interrupted the conversation of the diners. The French developed the idea of adding an extra cover to the edge of the table. This was easier to remove, so it could be quickly exchanged for a clean one during the meal without having to clear the rest of the table. The term "cover" is still used in restaurants today to indicate the number of diners at a table. It was not long before these covers became detached from the table and were being used as napkins in the way we know today.

Napkin fashion

By the beginning of the 17th century elaborate neck ruffs were in fashion and needed protection from spills. Instead of being laid on people's knees, napkins began to be tied around their necks, becoming ever more generously sized as the ruffs became more flamboyant. The fashion conscious and the wealthy needed the largest napkins to ensure that their ostentatious neckwear was kept stain-free.

Guests became responsible for their own napkins, choosing them to suit the size of their ruffs. Naturally, the larger the ruff the larger the napkin had to be, and over time enormous napkins became an unlikely status symbol. As fashion changed and ruffs disappeared, giving

Left *Historically cutlery, glassware and china have always been set according to a formal pattern, which ensured that the meal was served with little hindrance to diners and servers.*

way to subtler collars, hosts resumed the responsibility of providing napkins, but they lost none of their status in the process.

By the end of the 17th century, it was not just size that mattered; shape was also important. Napkins were folded into ever more ornate shapes. Fans, flowers, birds and even heraldic devices graced the smartest tables. There were special folds for gentlemen and more elaborate folds for ladies. At really smart functions, each place was given its own individual fold. The competition between hosts became so intense that London butlers were sent to Paris to learn the latest styles and perfect their folding skills.

In the elegant Georgian period fashions became much more restrained and the elaborate folding of napkins fell out of favour, as it was considered far too fussy. It was not until the mid-19th century, with the rise of the middle classes, that the fashion was resurrected, as people sought to achieve new heights of gentility. But by the end of the Victorian era, fancy folding was again regarded as a little vulgar – as was the

custom of putting napkins on side plates, which was considered to mean that the host was showing off the fine china of the main plates. Nevertheless, the classic folds have survived and can still be used to great effect to give an air of elegance and style to formally dressed tables, worthy of the grandest occasions.

Above *Dressing the table for even the simplest occasion suggests a certain formality about dining, presentation of food and expected codes of behaviour.*

Left *A picnic is a social occasion at which a napkin is an essential item of tableware.*

Napkin etiquette

The first rule with napkins is that they should be provided: as the host it is your responsibility to see that each of your guests is equipped with a freshly laundered napkin to protect their clothes and wipe their fingers. Etiquette decrees that there are napkins to suit different types of occasion and event.

What to use when

Afternoon tea, a popular meal through the 19th and 20th centuries and still a delightful way to entertain today, is the occasion on which the smallest and prettiest napkins should be brought out. Because it is seen mainly as a ladies' or children's occasion, napkins for afternoon tea have traditionally been made of delicate materials, such as fine lawn, exquisitely embroidered and measuring a tiny 20–30cm/8–12in square.

For the cocktail hour, which became popular early in the 20th century, small napkins made of gossamer fabrics such as lace, organza and fine cotton lawn became popular as the kind to hand out to catch drips from glasses and wipe fingers clean as the canapés were passed around. While such conventions need no longer be followed, they can add to the sense of occasion and help to set the party mood.

The general rule for napkins is: the less formal the occasion, the smaller and more decorated the napkin can be. Dinner napkins should be generously proportioned – up to 1m/1yd square – and should be used folded in half, adequately covering the most ample lap with a double thickness of good quality fabric. For less formal dinners you can use smaller napkins, about 75cm/30in square, but no smaller than 50cm/20in square.

Below A white dinner napkin over a waiter's arm looks smart, while protecting his clothes and providing an instant cloth with which to wipe any spills.

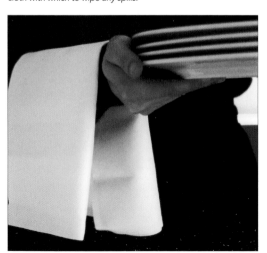

Below A napkin wrapped around the neck of a wine bottle will catch any drips as the wine is poured. It also makes holding a chilled wine or champagne bottle easier.

Right Table linen was traditionally always white. A white setting makes the table look formal and neat, while displaying many styles of tableware to its best advantage.

For most entertaining we are much more relaxed than our forebears; while white napkins remain the classic choice, patterns and colours are suitable for all but the most formal of occasions. If you keep a selection of different types, varying in size, colour and material, you are bound to be able to fit the right style to every occasion, especially if you customize them with some of the many ideas in this book.

Managing your napkin

Even today, when many of the fussier aspects of table manners have been abandoned in favour of a general awareness of the comfort of your fellow diners, there are still some formal occasions when elaborate etiquette will be observed.

At formal dinners and banquets one of the first stumbling blocks can be deciding when to unfold your napkin. In top hotels and restaurants around the world the waiters often deal with this: once everyone is seated they may go around the table, unfolding the napkins and either handing them to each guest or flicking them into their laps. If this is not done for you, wait at least until everyone is seated before unfolding your napkin, but make sure it is on your lap just as the first course arrives.

Large dinner napkins should be left folded in half, so there is a double thickness on your lap, and small napkins completely unfolded. The napkin should be left on your lap throughout the meal, except when you need to lift it to wipe your mouth. In parts of France some people still tuck their napkins into their collars, and this is perfectly proper, although in other countries at more formal occasions it may seem a little eccentric.

If, during a formal dinner, your napkin slithers off your lap, do not attempt to dive down under the table to rescue it from among other diners' feet. Attract the attention of a waiter, who will either retrieve the napkin or bring a fresh one.

When it is time to get up at the end of the meal, put your napkin on the table. In Europe it is usual to leave the napkin crumpled on the table to indicate that it is ready for laundering. In America it is more correct to leave it neatly folded. At family meals you should fold your napkin when you have finished with it, or roll it up and replace it in your napkin ring, before leaving the table, even if it needs laundering.

Using napkins

The way people eat has changed dramatically over the centuries: we may no longer spear a chicken on a knife or tear it apart with our fingers like a medieval banqueter, but nor do we feel the need to eat a banana with a knife and fork or serve lamb chops dressed with little paper frills, as was à la mode a few generations ago. However, while fashions in etiquette come and go, napkins remain a basic adjunct of our eating habits, and not only at the dinner table. Even if you're just eating a sandwich on the beach or a burger at a street party, a napkin comes in useful – though it's most likely to be a paper one.

Eating at the table

For everyday family meals, napkins are there to wipe fingers and mouths and protect everyone's clothes. Unless they get dirty during a meal they can be folded or rolled up ready for next time, and named or monogrammed napkin rings mean that everyone knows which one is theirs.

At formal meals, when your guests are dressed in their best clothes, they'll appreciate large dinner napkins that sit securely in their laps just in case of drips and spills. When you're serving

wine, wrapping a napkin round the bottle will stop condensation or iced water from a chilled bottle trickling on to your guests as you fill their glasses, or drips of red wine staining the tablecloth. Luxurious, thick napkins can be helpful when handing round hot dishes or plates, or lifting the lids of hot dishes, and you can also use their insulating properties by tucking them around a batch of hot bread rolls or tortillas. If you're serving food that is to be eaten with the fingers, it's a good idea to provide paper as well as fabric napkins, but bear in mind that the fabric ones may get quite dirty too, and replacements may be welcomed for the remainder of the meal.

When buying or making fabric napkins, it's worth bearing all these possible uses in mind, as it's clear that there are advantages to having a generous number in each set. Allow for plenty of matching spares for tasks such as wrapping bottles, lining baskets for bread or fruit, or supplying replacements if napkins get lost under the table or have to be used to mop up a spill.

Barbecues and picnics

Most outdoor eating tends to be fairly informal, but people still like to be able to wipe their fingers. Barbecue food is not only sticky but also hot, so plenty of napkins will protect fingers and clothes and can even be used as impromptu tablecloths on the grass or the beach. A roll of paper towels may be practical when you're eating outdoors (and you should certainly have

Left Napkins wrapped around hot serving dishes can be used to match the setting of the day, while protecting your hands from the heat.

Right *For serve-yourself buffet-type functions leave a pile of napkins with the plates so that guests can help themselves.*

Below *For outdoor eating individually wrap a place setting of knife, fork and spoon in its own napkin. That way the cutlery won't get lost in transit and every guest will be catered for.*

and fruit – much more picturesque and appetizing than plastic bags and boxes. A really grand picnic deserves to be eaten from proper china rather than paper plates, so use napkins to protect the crockery while travelling to the picnic spot.

On a smaller scale than the classic picnic hamper, a small basket lined with a colourful napkin can turn a simple offering of food, such as a pie for an elderly relative or some fruit from your garden for a new neighbour, into a delightful gift.

Treats on trays

Half the fun of taking someone breakfast in bed is in the setting of the tray: the best china, a flower or two, some delicious food, and of course, a pretty napkin to complete the picture – and perhaps another to line the tray. This kind of attention to detail can also help to cheer someone up when they're ill in bed or just languishing on the sofa. Even if they don't feel like eating much they'll appreciate the trouble you've taken.

one handy), but it's so much more fun to unpack a picnic hamper in which the food is excitingly hidden under bright, colourful cotton napkins. Hearty, overfilled French bread sandwiches can be individually wrapped in napkins to hold them together and contain the crumbs, and you can also use napkins to parcel up home-made cakes

Placing and presenting napkins

Crisp, freshly laundered napkins are an essential feature of every well-set table. They may be pressed in large, plain squares and laid at each place with the minimum of fuss, or folded in a variety of ways to complement the meal and the style of the table setting, using some of the ingenious ideas presented in this book.

Traditionally, a plainly folded napkin is placed in the centre of each place setting, between the knife and fork. However, if you plan to put the first course of a meal on the table before everyone is seated, the folded napkin would go to the left of the place setting, on the side plate, in which case you would probably fold it into an oblong or triangle, or roll it. A complex, sculptural fold can be placed in the centre of a dinner plate, or may be designed to occupy a bowl or a glass. Napkins can also be arranged to hold a set of cutlery, chopsticks, a place card, a flower, or even a small gift. Whatever the arrangement, make sure your assemblage is quick and easy to dismantle when the meal begins.

On a buffet table, it's best to stack napkins simply and provide a generous amount: bear in mind that guests rarely retain their napkins after the main course and many may take a second one with their dessert. Roll a napkin around each knife and fork, or pile the napkins in a basket near the plates and cutlery.

Simple presentation

If your table setting is very elaborate, with flowers at each place and spectacular china and glassware, it's often best to keep the napkin folds simple, and this is obviously appropriate for

Above *For a large buffet gathering, wrap each individual set of cutlery in its own napkin so that guests can take their own once they have served themselves from the buffet.*

informal occasions. But they should still be impeccably clean and pressed. To form a neat square, press the napkin, making sure all the corners are true. Fold it in half and then in half again, pressing each fold. It may be laid square or at a diagonal between the knife and fork. If you are using very large napkins, it may be better to fold them in thirds in each direction to make a square of the perfect size – this takes some practice.

To make a triangle, fold the square diagonally and press the fold. Lay the napkin on a side plate with the long side nearest the fork, or on a plate in the middle of the setting.

A simple oblong made by folding a square in half is an ideal way to display a napkin with a decorative or monogrammed corner. Alternatively, with plain napkins folded and pressed into quarters, opposite sides of the square may be folded underneath and pressed to make an oblong shape. Lay the short side with the hemmed edge at the bottom of the setting.

Rolled napkins, secured with rings or tied with ribbon or cord, will sit neatly in place if they are laid on the table or plate with the edge of the roll underneath.

Tips for successful folding

For the best results, use heavy linen napkins not less than 45cm/18in square. The napkins must be cut square and the fabric must be cut straight on the weave, so that it will not easily pull out of shape. Linen for folding should be washed, starched and ironed while damp. Gently pull the napkin back into shape if necessary as you iron, to ensure it is perfectly square.

Iron on a large surface – an ironing board can be too narrow when pressing large napkins. Use a table instead, protecting the surface with a thick, folded towel covered with a piece of plain white cotton. Dampen napkins that have dried before ironing. Use traditional starch (spray starch will not give a sufficiently crisp finish). Traditional starch may be mixed and sprayed on linen using a clean plant spray. Allow it to soak into the fabric for a minute or two before ironing.

When you are folding napkins into complicated shapes, press each fold individually for the best results; soft folds should not be pressed.

Below A white table setting with matching napkins suggests formality. Shaking out the napkin is a clear signal that the meal is about to commence.

Buying and choosing fabric

You cannot go wrong with plain white linen napkins. Freshly laundered and sweetly scented, they have been the correct choice for formal occasions since the 16th century. The finest napkins are made of silk damask – characterized by intricate designs incorporated into the weave – which was introduced into Europe from Damascus in the Middle East by returning Crusaders in the 12th century.

Once damask had arrived in Europe, textile workers in France, Flanders and Ireland learnt the weaving techniques and the designs used to make it, and applied them to linen, and later to cotton. Traditionally, a set of damask table linens embroidered with a family monogram formed part of a young woman's dowry, and damask remains the most popular choice for table napkins today.

Practical qualities

While starched white damask is perfect for the most formal meals, most entertaining today is far more relaxed. Napkins in deep colours or with all-over patterns can be used on almost any occasion, helping to create the mood and look you want for your table or party setting. But even if bright green or deep red napkins are key to the colour scheme of your table setting, don't forget that these objects are not just for looking at: napkins are first and foremost useful articles, and their tactile quality and absorbency is important.

Delicate little squares of lace or lawn make charming accessories for tea parties or cocktails, but for other occasions go for more substantial fabrics that will cope with spills and sticky fingers. Each guest will handle their napkin, even if only when laying it on their lap, so the fabric should be

Above *Damask cotton napkins with a woven pattern are hard-wearing and serviceable. These will last for years and washing will soften the woven fabric.*

Above *Antique lace-edged napkins are most likely to have been embroidered at home, and are valued for the quality of their workmanship. They can often be bought second-hand.*

a pleasure to touch. For this reason, it needs to be smooth and thick, and faultlessly pressed. Napkins of a generous size and weight not only feel better but are less likely to slip off people's knees and disappear under the table. On another practical note, it's vital to use fabric that's tough enough to stand up to rigorous washing: one good reason for the popularity of white linen and cotton is that they can be boiled or bleached to get rid of stains and give a scrupulously clean finish every time. If you are choosing coloured napkins, or fabrics for making your own, make sure they are colourfast and can be washed and ironed on hot settings.

For folding purposes, heavy linen is best, as it becomes firm and crisp when starched. Plain napkins should measure 45–50cm/18–20in square, or more, and this size is essential for many of the more complicated folds shown in this book. Otherwise, look for natural fabrics and good quality weaves that press beautifully and keep their shape. Woven stripes and checks will stay square and if you are making your own napkins the patterns act as useful guides for cutting and hemming.

Above *Good quality linen has an evenweave making it perfect to decorate with drawn thread work or with a bound edging.*

Paper napkins

For large parties and informal occasions such as barbecues, paper napkins are more practical than fabric ones. Make sure they are large and fairly thick. Fold them in half then fan them out in a large basket on a buffet table, perhaps folding one napkin into a water lily shape for the centre of the arrangement. When laying a garden table, allow two or three different coloured napkins for each place setting. Fan them simply or fold a pair in contrasting colours together in a water lily or roll-top design.

Right *Luxury fabrics add a special quality to a table setting.*

Japanese paper napkins, though fine and thin, are quite strong. They are often delicately patterned and may be round or square, with fluted or gilded edges. They can be used on their own, or in conjunction with fabric napkins if you have chosen a course for a formal meal that is eaten with the fingers. Fold them attractively with the fabric napkins; clear the paper napkins away with the plates before the next course.

Laundering and aftercare

Since the main raison d'être of table linen is to catch spills, stain removal has always been the first step in laundering. Modern proprietary stain removers followed by a machine wash have made this easier, but there are still particular stains that require a little attention.

Washing

Linen is strong, largely shrink-resistant, and can be safely washed at 60°C/140°F, which effectively washes out most food stains. Densely woven white cottons can also be washed at 60°C/140°F, though looser weaves, coloureds and polyester mixes should be laundered at no more than 40°C/100°F.

Pressing

The key to getting the best from any napkin is in the starching and pressing. A well-starched napkin holds its folds the best, and perfectionists will add traditional starch to the rinsing water.

LAUNDRY SYMBOLS

WASHING

 The number inside the wash tub symbol indicates the maximum centigrade temperature you can used using a normal wash cycle.

 A single bar below the wash tub symbol indicates a gentler washing action. This symbol is used for synthetic fabrics.

 Two bars under the wash tub symbol indicates the wool wash so a delicate cycle should be used.

 This symbol is used for hand wash garments only. The label will give other details such as temperature, drying and ironing.

 A crossed out wash tub indicates dry cleaning only.

DRY CLEANING

 A P indicates that certain solvents are suitable.

 A bar under a circle indicates the garment is sensitive to some dry cleaning processes.

 An A means that all solvents normally used for dry cleaning are suitable.

 A crossed out circle shows that the garment is not suitable for dry cleaning.

IRONING

 Three dots indicate the hotest setting on an iron.

 Two dots indicate the medium heat setting.

 The iron with one dot is used for synthetic fabrics.

 A crossed out iron means do not iron.

TUMBLE DRY

 This symbol indicates that the garment may be tumble dried.

 A single dot means the garment should be dried on the lowest heat setting.

 Two dots indicate that the garment can be dried on the high heat setting.

 A crossed out symbol means the garment is not suitable for tumble drying.

 This symbol indicates the garment should be dried flat away from direct heat.

BLEACHING

 A triangular symbol refers to chlorine bleach only.

A crossed out triangle means do not use chlorine bleach.

Nowadays few of us have the time for traditional starching. However you can quickly achieve similar results by stretching the still damp napkins into shape, then pressing them using a little spray starch and a non-steam iron on a hot setting. Start by pressing on the reverse side to avoid any watermarks and to remove most of the creases, then on the right side, to enhance the linen's natural sheen. Re-press any napkins flat before making any of the napkin folds.

Left Drying linens over lavender bushes is an old-fashioned but easy way to add scent to your laundry. Choose a day when the linen won't blow away.

Above Linen should be stored in a clean and dry cupboard. If it is linen that is used infrequently, adding sprigs of herbs will keep it smelling fresh for the next occasion when it is used.

Storing

Linens were once stored in airing cupboards with slatted shelves to allow plenty of ventilation to the fabric and to prevent mildew and damp from occuring. They were also often scented with lavender, which is a natural antiseptic and insect repellent. Nowadays, with central heating, our houses are much drier and most of us do not have the same problems with mildew and damp, so linens can safely be kept in drawers and cupboards with solid shelves. Few of us have time to make scented lavender bags but the increasingly popular modern alternative is to use scented ironing water (there's plenty of lavender- or rose-scented water available) and then to line drawers with scented drawer liners, ensuring linens stay fresher for longer. Alternatively you could buy ready-made herb bags.

STAIN REMOVAL

Candle wax
Scrape off any excess. Sandwich the stained area between two pieces of blotting paper or brown wrapping paper, then press using a warm, dry iron. The wax will melt and be absorbed by the paper.

Red wine
There are two traditional methods of removing red wine. Treat immediately – while you are still at the table, depending on the formality of the occasion. First, soak up the spill with a kitchen towel. Then either douse the red wine with white wine and the stain should disappear, or sprinkle on a thick layer of salt, to soak up the wine.

Spicy food
This can be stubborn and often bleach may be the only answer. Start by trying a stain remover. If you are still left with a stain, soak white cloths in a bleach solution of 1 tablespoon of bleach to 1 litre (1¾ pints) of water. Launder as normal.

Scorch marks
The use of a hot iron to press napkins means they are vulnerable to scorch marks. Avoid this by ironing while still damp and by keeping the iron moving. If a napkin does become scorched, soak it in cold milk as soon as possible, or soak in a bleach solution of 1 tablespoon of bleach to 1 litre (1¾ pints) of water.

Napkins for all occasions

From ritzy cocktail parties to friendly suppers, and from formal weddings to picnics on the beach – wherever there is food or drink, napkins are needed. Here you will find ideas to match the napkin to the event.

Inspirational ideas

Whether you're using dramatic coloured linens or classic white damask, table napkins are an important part of the whole decorative scheme, adding strong colour and texture or striking a formal note. You need to plan the colour and style of your table setting as a whole, carrying a theme through and making sure it harmonizes with the room's décor, the occasion and the food.

Above *Thick, crisp linen looks fabulous in strong colours that bring out its texture.*

Above *Hide neatly folded napkins in smart tracing paper envelopes.*

Above *For a celebration table, place a few elegant dragées inside each napkin.*

Above *Loosely tuck folded napkins into glasses to add height to the tablesetting.*

Above *For an oriental feel, tie napkins with natural string and curtain weights.*

Above *Enfold pre-starter nibbles in pure white napkins on each side plate.*

Above *Beautiful colour-matching of accessories makes a very elegant table.*

Above *Delicately patterned china and pale linens create a period look.*

Above *A well co-ordinated green theme gives a calm, mellow look to the table.*

Above *Bend a piece of silver wire into a simple heart shape and entwine with red wool for a charming Valentine's day decoration.*

Above *Antique green plates and white table linen strike a fresh, outdoor note that is perfect for lunch on a summer's day.*

Above *The classic combination of blue and white is timeless, whatever the style.*

Above *Use white linens with silver and coloured filmy ribbons for a christening.*

Above *Accessorize with white daisies to complete a fresh, summery table.*

Weddings

Memorable and romantic, wedding tables have a lot to live up to. The bride needs to adore the look you create because it is, after all, her day. Yet the decorations need to appeal to guests of every generation.

Flowers will be an important part of the table decorations, and the colour scheme chosen for these can be carried through into the trimmings of napkins to give a co-ordinated look, perhaps using some of the same flowers. Many brides like to add a pretty bonbonnière or favour for each guest, and these could be tucked into each napkin as a surprise.

White napery is the safest route to follow, but this need not limit you to a traditional look. White can look equally good in a sleek minimalist setting, with the flowers and napkin ties providing accent colours.

Left *Crisp white napkins are given the romantic treatment with a single deep pink rose (which sweetly matches the pattern of the traditional china) tucked into a delicate lilac organza bow.*

Above *Delightfully feminine and undeniably bridal, this rolled napkin has been tied with a generous organza bow. Small hedgerow flowers tucked into the fold look simple and pretty and evoke sweet-smelling summer meadows.*

Above *A neatly folded napkin tied with narrow ribbon makes an elegantly restrained statement. Tuck in a sprig of a fragrant herb, such as lavender or rosemary, that will not wilt during the meal.*

Right *Champagne, candelabras and sparkling glassware set the celebratory tone of this classic wedding table. The deep pink roses at each place setting look simple and fresh as well as being unashamedly romantic. Their strong colour is carried along the snowy white tablecloth by a seemingly artless scattering of matching petals.*

Celebrate in style

Significant events such as anniversaries or naming ceremonies deserve a degree of formality that lends importance to the occasion. A good starting point is to work out a colour scheme that complements both the event and the room, and creates a sense of harmony. The style of the table setting will also depend on the age of the guest or guests of honour: for a golden wedding or eightieth birthday you will probably want to set the table in a classic style, with white napery and the family silver, whereas for an engagement party a bold, modern theme would be appropriate, and for a christening you might want to use baby pinks or blues.

Choose napkins, china and glassware that suit the occasion, picking up the tones of the furniture and décor, and accentuate your scheme with a clever choice of flowers.

Left A single pink hydrangea floret laid casually on each folded napkin adds a finishing touch that will charm guests of any age at a special family meal.

Above Purple anemones set off the deep blue plates and tone with the lilac chair covers. For this elegant formal scheme the linen napkins have been very simply folded.

Above This exquisitely pretty floral theme, with the warm pink of the china matched by the ebullient hydrangea flowers, is perfectly set off by classic monogrammed damask napkins.

Family lunch

Delicious food, simply prepared and set out on a table laid with colourful linen and earthenware crockery, sets the ambience for a warm, friendly family get-together. You'll want to keep the mood very informal for a relaxed atmosphere, but a prettily laid table will help to give the meal a sense of occasion. Whether you eat around a big kitchen table or outside in the garden, bright, homespun cotton or linen napkins provide bright accents of colour while maintaining the casual, easy-going style.

If you are hosting a buffet or barbecue, plenty of napkins are still a good idea; you can use them to mop up spills and to wipe children's sticky hands and faces.

Below *Folksy cotton tablecloths and napkins are perfect for family meals around the kitchen table, with pretty embroidered details to add charm and interest.*

Above *Take inspiration from the Mediterranean, where they know how to turn a family meal into a party. Spread a colourful, country-style cloth and add napkins in toning colours.*

Above *Instead of folding crisp linen napkins, bring out the casual style of the meal by tying each one into a loose, chunky knot to give the table setting an impromptu look.*

Supper for friends

Entertaining nowadays is easy, informal and relaxed. Simple dishes made with delicious fresh ingredients can be quickly put together and laid out on platters for a meal that is a visual delight.

Avoid making the table setting too fussy; it doesn't matter if you don't own enough matching plates or napkins to cater for all your guests, simply mix up what you have, then pile them high for an abundant look. The key is to keep to a colour theme: all white, perhaps, so you can mix old and new. Alternatively, you could assemble shades that are tonally compatible or, on the more adventurous side, those that contrast. If you need to use china and glassware that mix a lot of different colours and patterns, you can help to create a sense of harmony on the table by choosing a linking shade in the fabric of the tablecloth and the napkins.

Above By keeping to an all-white scheme when catering for a large number, your table will always look coordinated, however many different sets of china and napery you need to use.

Above Even the simplest table setting can be given a dash of contemporary style, and a seasonal accent, with the addition of a single flower from the garden.

Left Cottons and linens in woven stripes create a rustic mood for impromptu meals. Over the years, with repeated laundering, these traditional fabrics take on a beautiful softness.

The cocktail hour

Recreate the pure glamour of the jazz age in your own home with an impeccably organized cocktail party, with everyone dressed in their best, a generous selection of classic cocktails, and irresistible nibbles circulating freely.

For a cocktail party to run really smoothly, you need to pay special attention to the practicalities. With everyone standing around, glass in hand, there are bound to be a few inelegant spills, so equip both your guests and the servers with suitable small-scale napkins that are as elegant as the occasion. Hark back to the heyday of the formal cocktail party with beautifully embroidered and crisply starched napkins of miniature dimensions. If you can find cocktail-sized vintage napkins with deliciously thick embroidery or Art Deco trimmings they'll really help to set the correct retro tone for the occasion.

Right *The fuss-free simplicity of these pure white linen napkins looks ultra-chic with the geometric lines of classic Martini cocktail glasses.*

Left *Guests can use small cocktail napkins under their glasses as refills are poured to catch any spills or drips.*

Above *A delicately embroidered napkin tucked into each champagne glass (with a pretty swizzle stick) strikes a lovely whimsical note for guests at a proper cocktail party.*

Afternoon tea

Tea served in the drawing room, or under a leafy tree in the garden, with fine bone china cups and saucers, thinly cut sandwiches and luscious home-made cakes, is a meal that speaks of a bygone age and a more leisurely lifestyle than most of us enjoy nowadays. However, it's fun to recreate this mood sometimes, and a charming way to entertain weekend guests.

Everything on the tea table needs to be delicately pretty, and dainty napkins with floral embroidery or lacy edgings are a must, to go with your best floral china tea service.

Left *Delicious home-made chocolate biscuits are prettily decorated for a special tea and presented on a faultlessly starched linen napkin.*

Above *A cool green and white jacquard-woven linen napkin goes perfectly with this traditional flowered bone china tea set, arranged on a wicker tray ready for tea in the garden.*

Above *Delicate crystallized rose petals are the romantic finishing touch on these lovely home-made biscuits for a special tea, and their pretty colour is echoed in the pink and white napkins.*

Above *In a more contemporary take on the traditional floral theme, this funky striped china is accompanied by napkins in a bold printed cotton with large-scale flowers.*

A summer picnic

Arrange a memorable summer outing with friends and family by packing a picnic to take to a glorious secluded corner of the countryside, or simply carry your meal out into the garden. Dainty, floral-patterned cotton table linen evokes summer meadows and will happily mix and match with striped cloths in similar tones.

Your delicious picnic fare will be even more enticing and appetizing if you pack it into a traditional wicker hamper. Include a colourful tablecloth to spread on the grass for your feast, and use co-ordinating napkins to wrap loaves, home-made pies and fruit.

Above *Stuff crusty baguettes with tempting fillings and wrap each in a colourful napkin to keep them fresh and make them easy to hold at your picnic.*

Above *A brightly striped tablecloth teamed with pretty floral napkins sets the scene for a picnic lunch in the garden. A jugful of summer flowers turns it into a special occasion.*

Above *Load the car with a colourful rug and a groaning hamper, with delicious food wrapped in colourful napkins, and set off for a perfect summer picnic in the countryside.*

A beach party

Sea air can be guaranteed to give everyone a hearty appetite, the perfect excuse for lunch at the beach. You can put up a beach umbrella and spread your picnic rug on the sand, but a long, lazy lunch can be so much more pleasurable when set up on a trestle table with some folding chairs away from the crowds. Set it with plain napkins and unbreakable enamelware, and choose seaside shades of blues and aquas teamed with plenty of white to keep the look fresh. Even on the warmest, sunniest days, you'll need to go prepared to cope with the elements: linens need to be anchored down on breezy beaches, so before you set the table scour the shore for attractive pebbles to keep each napkin decoratively in its place.

Right *For a delightfully simple lunch on the beach, put your picnic in a sturdy hamper and eat it while on the sand or in a deckchair. Lining the basket with a colourful cotton napkin will help to keep the sand out of your food.*

Above *A blue and white colour scheme is always successful at the seaside: stripes and checks look clean and fresh and go perfectly with enamel plates and sun-bleached paintwork.*

Above *If you put each filled baguette in a different colour napkin there's no arguing about whose is whose – so children can nibble their lunch before rushing off, then come back for more later on.*

Left *Tablecloths and napkins will need anchoring to stop them being blown around by a stiff sea breeze.*

Outdoor living

When summer comes the garden can be turned into an outdoor room, and every meal of the day can be eaten at the garden table in a relaxed and less formal manner. There's no reason why it shouldn't be as attractive as your table indoors, with a jug of flowers, tablecloths and napkins, pretty crockery and glassware, and candles in the evening.

Choose table linens in bright fresh colours that will look good in bright sunlight, or in the cool green shade of a leafy tree, and easy cotton fabrics like seersucker patterned with gingham. If your garden furniture is painted, seek out napkins and crockery that suit its colour scheme to create an idyllic garden picture that will give you pleasure on every warm day of the year.

Right When the garden is full of flowers in the summer, don't forget to pick some to decorate the table. These deep purple geraniums look wonderful with blue napkins and plates.

Above White place mats and neatly folded white napkins, with elegant plates and glassware, can create an effective setting for a formal meal on the garden terrace.

Above Even if you're not going out for a picnic, you can create a lunch to remember by packing a basket with fresh food and lemonade and carrying it to the bottom of the garden.

Festive occasions

Buying special Christmas tableware can be an extravagance that proves too costly for the time of year. Plan, instead, to add festive touches with napkins and accessories that add the glamour and glitter. This is the time of the year when you can go over the top with gold and silver to bring sparkle to the festivities.

While you're unlikely to own a whole dinner service that is specially decorated for Christmas, it can be a joy to collect a few items of tableware that are unpacked at this one time of year – a glass dessert dish sprinkled with gold stars, or a cake stand wreathed with holly. A set of beautiful linen napkins embroidered with Christmas motifs would be a pleasure to make and could become a well-loved feature on your festive table, one of your family's Christmas traditions.

Left Deep, rich colours with some added sparkle conjure up the spirit of Christmas as a time of light and warmth in a cold, dark season.

Left Ties of golden cord with tasselled ends lend an elegant touch of classic Christmas glamour to a set of antique monogrammed damask napkins.

Above A pure white table setting is a wonderfully delicate festive touch with a simple ivy leaf decoration at each place and a collection of sparkling Venetian coloured glasses.

Above A gold and white scheme, with touches of traditional Christmas greenery, allows you to create a table with plenty of glamour and sparkle without going over the top.

Easter

A party table for an Easter meal is the perfect setting for a celebration of the beginning of a new season after the long, dark winter months. As the sunlight strengthens, your table can reflect the freshness of the outdoor scene with clear greens, pinks and yellows. An artlessly arranged mixture of bright daffodils, tulips and hyacinths – perhaps brought straight in from the garden – will bring the scent of spring into the room and make a beautiful Easter centrepiece with a pretty basket of traditionally decorated eggs.

Choose napkins for your Easter table in pretty flower colours, or fresh stripes or prints. Tie them with ribbons and tuck a few primroses into each knot, or fold them loosely and hide a tiny Easter treat inside, such as a foil-covered chocolate rabbit or a few speckled candy eggs.

Above right Coloured sugar mice peeping out of cones of felt in contrasting shades make an Easter table decoration that will enchant children of all ages.

Below The classic colour scheme of blue and white is full of the appeal of the new season, and can be given a special twist for the Easter table with an original collection of stencilled eggs.

Above Nestle a little posy of spring flowers such as primulas from the garden into each napkin for seasonal appeal and a focus of fresh colour.

Whites

Whatever the style of your décor, you can always be confident that white will work on the table. Extremely elegant, it is the darling of top chefs because it complements all types of food perfectly. At home, white table linens will prove a good investment because you can mix, match and add to your collection over the years.

If you only ever buy one set of napkins, pure white linen or double damask has to be the best choice. This may appear to be extravagant at the time, but both launder beautifully, and will retain their quality no matter how much you use them. If anything they will improve with age, and you may prefer to hunt for a set of antique linen, with neatly hand-stitched hems and embroidery.

Choose pure whites for sophistication, perhaps adding exquisitely scented flowers to the setting, or use creamy white napkins for warm elegance.

Above *The elegant appearance of smooth blue-white porcelain is perfectly offset by the textural contrast provided by these elaborately pleated white napkins.*

Above *With an all-white setting, interesting textures come to the fore: these crisply woven drawn-threadwork napkins in off-white look gorgeous tied simply with ordinary household string.*

Right *The colour and style of this modern creamy-white china is perfectly matched by contemporary linens in a plain but textured weave.*

Brights

For an instant change of mood on your table that will have a powerful influence on the look of the whole room, add a splash of colour. Fashion has come off the catwalk to influence interiors, and if you want to set your table with your current favourite shade, the easiest way to do it is to indulge yourself with some bright new napkins. Many high-street stores stock inexpensive cotton sets in all the latest hues, or, failing that, you could just buy a metre of fabric in the perfect colour and cut out and stitch your own napkins. They will probably cost you less than a vase of flowers, and they create instant impact.

If you have coloured china, find a perfect match or go for a strong contrast. In a neutral, minimalist, setting, you could also have fun with a multi-coloured set in hot orange, pink and red, or strong blues and yellows.

Above *Vibrant contrasting colours with touches of gold embroidery give your table setting an Indian flavour.*

Above *Mix napkin colours with confidence by picking out some of the tones in a patterned or striped tablecloth.*

Above *A glorious mixture of warm, deep colours, unified by carefully selected detailing, creates a sumptuous effect.*

Above *Traditional Provençal printed cottons, in sun-drenched colours and simple designs, give the table a bright summery feel.*

Pastels

Sweetly pretty pastel colours add a friendly touch to your table, softening and warming the severity of a white tablecloth. They are easy on the eye and a positive pleasure. Use a single colour to set a mood, or play around with a mixture of delicate shades to create a table setting with the charm of a bowl of sugared almonds.

While deep, strong colours are at their best on a candlelit dinner table, pastels are the soft fresh colours of daylight. Apple blossom pink, primrose yellow or the palest greens echo the colours of the garden and are perfectly matched with delicate flowers, whether arranged as a centrepiece or held individually with ribbons or ties on each napkin. Use pastel-coloured napkins with plain white china and fine clear glassware for the most subtle effects.

Above Tucking pastel napkins into transparent white organza sachets adds translucency as just a hint of colour shows through, emphasized by tiny sprigs of fresh flowers.

Above Pale spring green looks wonderfully fresh on the table, especially when teamed with crockery in clear, glowing colours, bringing a feeling of the outdoors to the table.

Above Warm pink is a summery colour and a delightful foil for the fresh greens of fruits and salads, making the meal a visual delight as well as an appetizing feast.

Neutrals

The colours of the earth, from palest bone white to dark peat brown, mix naturally together to make a harmonious whole. Used for a table setting, this tranquil palette is an appropriate backdrop for delicious meals of wholesome, organic food. Yet neutrals are completely in tune with modern interiors, and just as much at home in a chic city environment as on a rustic scrubbed kitchen table.

The soft colour variations of undyed homespun linen are a perfect match for its knobbly, crunchy texture. Set it against smooth white plates on a plain tablecloth, and accessorize neutral napkins with rings and ties of natural materials such as rough sisal string. You could edge white cotton napkins with bands of grey or brown to give your table a cool, urban look.

Above This beautiful antique French napkin, in creamy white enhanced by a soft red stripe, has been neatly folded and fastened by cord wound around a matching pair of bone buttons.

Above The muted shading of natural, undyed linen is perfectly matched by trimmings drawn from the natural world: a simple wicker ring and a selection of subtly striped feathers.

Above An elegantly simple basketwork knot is secured by a fascinating bone tag, whose sparing decoration and smooth surface contrasts beautifully with the homespun napkin.

Florals

No table is complete without a simple arrangement of flowers to please the eye during a meal, and flowers have always been an intrinsic and important part of table decoration. They are a time-honoured motif for embroidery and textile printing, and floral designs on tablecloths can range from the discreet, stylized patterns of white damask to bold full-blown printed roses or embroidered designs of tiny sprigs and trailing stems. Printed or painted on a tea set, floral patterns evoke a gentler age of afternoon tea taken from fine bone china cups.

Floral prints make enchanting napkins, especially when the colours are light and bright and the designs are daintily small. Team them with old-fashioned china, such as an antique flower-strewn tea set or a traditional blue and white striped breakfast service.

Right *These hydrangea florets are a perfect match for the delicate willow green of the napkin, and make an ideal flower decoration for a simple raffia tie.*

Above *Floral patterns in table linens and china can be mixed together quite happily as long as you select colours of similar tones and patterns of comparable scale.*

Left *Any flower in pink or red, picked fresh from the garden makes a glorious table decoration in summer. Strengthen the visual effect with napkins of the same colour.*

Nature table

Work with the seasons to keep your table settings looking fresh and interesting. By taking inspiration from nature, the table will always look instinctively right, yet your decorations will often cost absolutely nothing as the raw materials are just outside your door.

The key to carrying off this effect successfully when decorating napkins is to add just the smallest sprig, or a single leaf, berry or flower to capture the essence of the natural scene, without gilding the lily. Keep your eyes open for interesting stems, pebbles, shells and feathers when you're out walking, and try to use other accessories that suit the mood of the season: tie napkins with sheer ribbons in pastel colours for spring, and bind them with sisal string or raffia in autumn to blend effectively with coloured leaves and springs of ripened berries.

Above *For a really charming summer table setting, make traditional chains of simple lawn daisies and other little flowers to dress bright napkins.*

Above *Add fallen leaves in tones of russet and orange to napkins in warm autumnal colours, and conjure up the season of mists and fruitfulness.*

Above *Add a delicate seasonal touch to a formal table design by weaving tiny sprigs of flowers into silver napkin rings around traditional damask napkins.*

Left *In winter, crisp red and white checked napkins look fabulous in a ring of woven twigs, entwined with a stem of ivy and a few red berries.*

Above *Striking leathery dark green leaves make dramatically shaped ties around pale napkins for a meal set on a shady table in the garden.*

Stripes and checks

There are fresh combinations of colours and patterns that are destined to never date. Used to decorate china, blue and white has managed to top the popularity stakes for more than 200 years since 18th-century Chinese imports inspired Josiah Spode to design the ever popular Willow Pattern. Unlikely to fall from favour now, this colourway is a useful linen cupboard mainstay, especially if you choose smart checks and stripes.

Other colours work equally well in these classic woven designs, and are easy to find whether you are buying new or antique textiles. You can build up a collection gradually, teaming windowpane weaves with smaller checks, and adding bold and narrow stripes. Don't worry if the colours are not an exact match, but bear in mind that while two different shades of the same colour could look like a mistake, three or more look planned.

Left Fabrics with woven stripes have a very traditional character. They always look smart and neat and fit easily into any setting and any colour scheme.

Above Checks in different sizes mix and match beautifully. Pick up the colour of the linens in the decoration of the tableware, as in the blue rims of these traditional enamelled plates.

Left A single pattern, such as this classic gingham check, gives a unifying theme to a collection of napkins, enabling you to mix together as many colours as you like for an original look.

Above *Although each of these napkins is a different colour they are recognizably a matching set, unified by their woven design of fine white stripes.*

Left *Bands of broad and narrow blue stripes on white linen napkins and dish towels are a classic style, equally at home in a country kitchen or a city flat. Matching striped linens with blue-striped white china gives a co-ordinated look.*

Above *A deep blue and white napkin in a contemporary style creates a very cool mood when combined with stark white plates and plain glasses on a bright white tablecloth.*

Above *Blue and white checks and stripes can be mixed endlessly and never fight with one another, so you can expand your collection over time with bric-à-brac finds.*

Antique

Old fabrics have a quality that is hard to match today, and antique linen that has been laundered many times has a softness and colour that is impossible to replicate. Many antique napkins are also beautifully decorated with drawn threadwork or embroidery, with handstitching of outstanding quality. If you enjoy hunting in antique shops and on bric-à-brac stalls, small-scale textiles of this kind are easily affordable and rewarding to collect. There's no need to buy a complete matching set. Old linens look wonderful when mixed together, so you can add to your collection whenever you see pieces you like, building up a unique harlequin set of beautiful napkins.

Above *This antique French dish towel has been folded to make a charming napkin "book" held in place by the string fastener, in which napkins can be kept until needed on the table.*

Above *An embroidered napkin is quickly turned into a charming pocket by turning in the corners and catching the edges in place. A flower-shaped button provides the finishing touch.*

Right *Mix and match antique napkins with an assortment of decorative finishes – their colour and the quality of the linen will ensure that they all look lovely together.*

Below *Whitework embroidery adds a luxurious touch to any place setting.*

Traditional

Classic and delicate china tableware, of the kind that we usually associate with a more traditional era and styling, has a charm of its own. With designs and colour schemes of every imaginable kind, napkins need to be carefully matched to ensure that colours and designs will not clash visually once on the table. For many designs, particularly old chinaware, plain white napkins may be the best choice. These may be embellished with embroidery, decorative scalloped edges or patterns in drawn threadwork. Very decorative napkins should be folded simply. If they have an embroidered monongram in one corner, fold them so that this is displayed. If you are trying to match new napkins to old china that has a busy pattern, try to match the colourway first, keeping the linen plain for visual simplicity and an elegant table setting.

Above Geometric patterns such as checks blend happily with a mixture of different floral prints if you choose designs that are of a similar scale and colour.

Below Plain white cotton or linen napkins are classic and timeless, decorated with traditional drawn threadwork. They are the perfect choice if you have tableware in elaborate floral designs.

Above Old-fashioned floral printed napkins have the right traditional feel for a well-appointed summer picnic: use them to line baskets for transporting china and food to your picnic spot.

Oriental tables

The simplicity and harmony of Oriental table settings provide a welcome antidote to today's increasingly demanding lifestyles: plain plates and folded napkins in neutral or earth colours are positioned with geometric rigour and little adornment on bare tables. If this is too stark for your taste, you could choose a white or neutral cloth and add a single flower or stem in a glass or porcelain vase, trimmed with a twist of raffia.

This elegant, restrained look can turn a quick stir-fry into a special occasion, although you do not have to wait until you are accomplished with a wok before you give it a try.

Strict attention to detail is the key to this look: everything on the table should be perfectly placed and aligned. Napkins need to be carefully pressed and beautifully folded or rolled, creating a sense of order and calm.

Above *Inspired by origami, this Japanese-style napkin fold has a sculptural look and its rolled central section makes a perfect holder for a place card and a tiny sprig of flowers.*

Above *A matt black bowl provides elegant contrast with a coarsely woven napkin in natural cream, precisely rolled. The beargrass-wrapped stone provides a touch of Japanese styling.*

Right *Classic white napkins are easily incorporated with a spare Oriental style if they are faultlessly pressed, simply folded or rolled and precisely placed on the table.*

Above *Chopsticks tied with raffia and placed with precision on toning napkins give a buffet party table an Eastern look, but you could achieve a similar effect with sets of knives and forks.*

Above *For a more relaxed, country style, still with an Oriental influence, combine bamboo-handled cutlery, woven rush plates and terracotta glazed bowls with neutral-coloured napkins.*

Above *The delicacy and fine lines of matt-textured Oriental porcelain is enhanced when accessorized with luxuriously thick table napkins in strong, earthy colours.*

Making and decorating napkins for all occasions

Exquisite edging, delicate embroidery, or a simple motif painted on to one corner can transform a simple square of fabric into a delightful napkin that is all the more gorgeous for the handcrafted detail. The joy is that napkins are small enough for an embroidery detail to be completed with gratifying speed.

Inspirational ideas

Easy edgings and simple decorative effects can transform plain napkins into something unique and special. Most involve only plain machine stitching or simple hand sewing, and none takes very long. You could also look for interesting ready-made trimmings and decorative materials such as ribbons and beads, or even little jewels to add a sparkle to your festive table.

Above *A little glass bead adds a different colour to a traditional cutwork daisy.*

Above *A border of self-coloured straight stitches finishes this napkin elegantly.*

Above *Linen and natural raffia make a great modern partnership.*

Above *Fine lilac organdie takes on a very feminine feel with this picot edging.*

Above *A narrow crochet trim is charming while avoiding any hint of frilliness.*

Above *Pretty shell discs on a ready-made trim are easy to sew on a toning napkin.*

Above *White lingerie trimmings have an alternative use adorning plain napkins.*

Above *Pearl buttons threaded on to plain household string make a stunning edging.*

Above *Four lines of straight stitching in blue look smart on plain white napkins.*

Above *A border of toile de jouy applied to linen napkins of a similar, but plain fabric gives a subtle but colourful effect.*

Above *Decorative satin ribbons can be used in all kinds of ways to add charming decoration to napkins.*

Above *The narrowest braid border adds richness to a linen napkin.*

Above *Nothing could be simpler than finishing plain napkins with frayed edges.*

Above *The beads on this coffee-coloured napkin set off the modern cutlery well.*

Making a plain napkin

If you need napkins in a specific colour or fabric, it can be easier and cheaper to buy a length of fabric and make your own. Choose linen or cotton in a firm, plain weave that will not pull out of shape, and follow the weave carefully when cutting out your squares.

MATERIALS

For each napkin:

- **Plain fabric 50cm/20in square**
- **Scissors**
- **Needle and tacking (basting) thread**
- **Sewing machine or needle and matching thread**

1 To cut out the napkin, snip into the selvage and pull a thread, then cut along the line. Measure 50cm/20in along the edge and repeat to cut the remaining sides of the square. Press under a narrow turning on each side, then press under a hem allowance of, say, 1cm/½in.

2 Unfold the pressed creases and turn the fabric in at 45 degrees at each corner so that the folds line up. Press each corner firmly to mark the diagonal line. Unfold the corners and trim them at 45 degrees, a short distance outside the diagonal crease.

3 Refold and press each of the creases then tack (baste) the hem and mitred corners in place. Stitch the hem by hand or machine. Slip stitch the mitres together, working from the corners inwards. Remove the tacking stitches and press.

Making a bound-edge napkin

A contrast binding is a classic way to finish the edge of a napkin. Use a fairly thin fabric to make the binding so that the finished corners are not too bulky and the binding can be easily stitched in place with a sewing machine. This is a very simple project to make.

   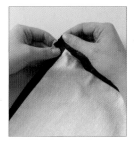

1 To cut the main fabric, snip into the selvage and pull a thread, then cut along the line. Measure 38cm/15in along the selvage and repeat the process. Measure along the cut edge and pull a thread to complete the square.

2 Press the strips for the binding in half lengthwise, with wrong sides together, then fold the long raw edges of each strip in to the centre and press again.

3 Place strips of binding down two opposite sides of the napkin and tack (baste) in place, checking that you catch the binding in the stitching on both sides. Stitch close to the folded edge.

4 Trim the ends of the binding flush with the edges of the napkin. Pin the other two pieces of binding in place. Turn the short ends in at the corners and tack. Stitch as before, reverse-stitching at each end.

MATERIALS

For each napkin:

- **38cm/15in square of fabric**
- **Scissors**
- **Measuring tape**
- **4 x 40cm/1½ x 16in of fabric for the binding**
- **Pins**
- **Needle and tacking (basting) thread**
- **Sewing machine and matching thread**

Cutlery roll

Smart braid and clever folding transform a plain napkin into a neat roll to hold a set of cutlery – perfect for picnicking. Cleverly accommodating a four-piece place setting plus acting as a napkin, the rolls can be filled up for each guest before setting out for your picnic, or stacked neatly on a buffet table.

MATERIALS

For each cutlery roll:

- 1 large napkin, 50cm/20in square
- 52cm/21in braid 4cm/1½in wide for binding
- Scissors
- Pins, needle and tacking (basting) thread
- Sewing machine and matching thread
- 2.7m/3yd matching braid 2cm/ ¾in wide for top edge, sides and ties

1 Cut a piece of the wider braid the same length as one side of the napkin. Place it along the edge of the napkin. Pin and tack (baste) in position, then machine stitch along both edges of the braid.

2 Place the napkin face down and fold up the braid-finished edge of the napkin to a depth that will hold the knife, fork and spoon. Cut two lengths of narrow braid to fit along the top edge of the roll. Pin one to the front of the top edge and the other to the back. Stitch through all three layers along both edges of the braid. Repeat with both side seams, tacking through all the layers to join the sides. Place the cutlery over the top of the folded edge and use pins to mark the positions of the stitching lines.

3 When you are happy with the spacing of the cutlery, tack the seams between the pockets and remove the pins. Machine stitch the seams, firmly securing each one at the top of the wide braid using a reverse stitch. Remove the tacking threads.

4 To make the ties, fold the remaining piece of narrow braid in half and pin in position halfway down one side between the two napkin layers. Stitch through all the layers along the narrow braid to join the seams. Turn in narrow double hems at the ends of the ties, and stitch.

Napkin pocket

Transform simple napkins into exquisite pockets for storing linens in scented cupboards or drawers. A plain piqué cotton napkin can be made to look very special with clever folding and the addition of an imaginative fastener. With the hems already finished off, there is little fiddly sewing to be done.

MATERIALS

- **White piqué napkin, approximately 45cm/18in square**
- **Needle and matching thread**
- **Ready-made rolled fastener**

1 Fold the napkin in half and then in half again, and run your thumb down the folds to make strong creases. Unfold, then fold the corners to the centre so they meet where the original creases cross. Make sure all the edges meet together accurately, then press.

2 Slip stitch the edges together down two sides of one point, leaving the opposite side open like the flap of an envelope. Make extra stitches where the corners meet, for extra strength.

3 Sew one part of the rolled fastener on to the loose flap and mark where it will join the other part of the fastener on the sewn section. Stitch the fastener firmly into position.

Drawn threadwork

For classic elegance, there is no better decoration for napkins than drawn threadwork. It is often used to stunning effect on banqueting linens. Choose an even-weave fabric that is made from strong fibres, otherwise they will keep snapping as you try to pull them out. Linen is ideal.

MATERIALS

For each napkin:

- **Linen 60cm/24in square**
- **Pins**
- **Needle and contrasting and matching threads**

1 Using pins, mark out lines 6cm/2½in in from each edge. Since the hem will be turned back to the drawn threadwork, this will give a finished border of 3cm/1¼in. Turn the hem back to the line of pins to check the result. Make a line of tacking (basting) stitches in contrasting thread in place of the pins.

2 Working inside the pinned area, carefully ease out one strand of the weave right the way across the fabric. Repeat this process, ensuring that the number of threads that are withdrawn is divisible by three. Repeat on all sides, pulling out an equal number of threads each time.

3 Turn in and press a narrow hem all around the raw edges, then fold this hemmed edge back to the line of withdrawn threads to make a double border. Press and tack in place. Mitre the corners (see Making a plain napkin). With the wrong side of the napkin towards you, work hem stitches, catching three threads at a time and taking in the edge of the hem as you go. Repeat all along the top edge of the drawn threads and then all along the lower edge, lining up the stitches to create a neat row of holes.

Appliqué napkin

Decorating with appliqué does not have to be intricate, complex or time-consuming. Even the simplest design, used to trim the edge of a napkin, can give it a more finished look. Use ready-made napkins or make them yourself from squares of fabric, and use the same fabric in a different colour for the appliqué.

MATERIALS

For each napkin:

- **Lime green napkin**
- **Scissors**
- **Tape measure**
- **Paper**
- **Needle and matching thread**
- **Yellow napkin**

1 Cut a 5cm/2in strip from the lime napkin. Fold the strip in half three times. Cut a piece of paper to the size of this quarter-fold, and then fold the paper in half and snip off one corner. Open out the paper and use it as a template to cut the corners of the folded lime strip. Open out the zigzag edging.

2 Turn in a 6mm/¼in hem along the long straight side of the lime strip and along the short ends. Press. Slip stitch the straight edge and the ends of the lime strip to the edges of the yellow napkin.

3 Slip stitch the zigzag edge of the strip to the napkin, turning in the edges as you go. You will need to turn in these edges only very slightly – just enough to neaten them – or you may find it difficult to create the points at the inner and outer corners of the zigzag.

Couched organza

Gossamer light and delicately translucent, organza has surprising body. It is naturally stiff, which means you can not only create light, luminous folds, but you can also crease it to a knife-edged sharpness. Couch a simple motif into one corner of each napkin for a pretty, embossed effect.

MATERIALS

- **Ready-made napkin in silk organza**
- **Tracing paper**
- **Fine felt-tipped pen**
- **Masking tape**
- **Dressmaking pencil**
- **Fine cotton string**
- **Needle and matching thread**
- **Scissors**

1 Press the napkin flat. Trace the motif from the back of the book using tracing paper and a felt-tipped pen. When the ink has completely dried, tape the motif on to a flat surface and place the hemmed napkin over the top, positioning the corner over the motif. Tape the napkin in position to fix both the tracing paper and the fabric firmly. Using a dressmaking pencil, trace the motif on to the corner of the napkin. Remove the masking tape securing the napkin.

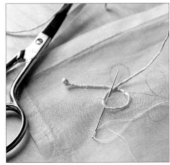

2 ◁ Knot the end of a piece of cotton string and lay the string along the traced design on the corner of the napkin. Using the needle and thread, neatly couch the string in position. When you near the end of the motif, make a knot at this end of the string, trim and stitch down neatly. Iron the couched motif string-side down on a towel, to avoid flattening the string.

Pearl-trimmed appliquéd cupids

If you want to create an outrageously romantic table dressing for a meal on a special Valentine's day or for a personal celebration, these engaging little cupids will provide a perfect finishing touch. Stitch them to the corners of silk organza napkins, then decorate their wings with tiny pearls.

MATERIALS

For each napkin:

- **50cm/18in square of white silk organza**
- **Pins**
- **Needle and white thread**
- **Tracing paper**
- **Pencil**
- **Paper**
- **Scissors**
- **Scrap of muslin or tulle**
- **6 seed-pearl beads**

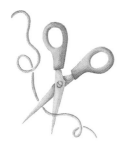

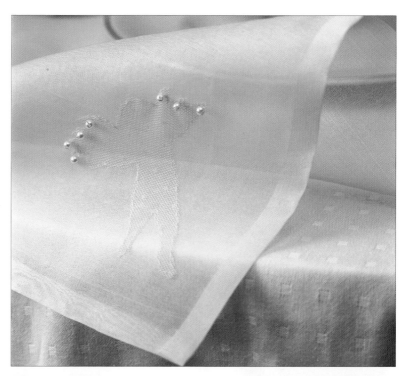

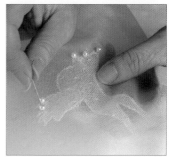

1 Turn in a narrow double hem all round the edge of the organza, press and slip stitch in place, mitring the corners. Trace the cupid at the back of the book and cut out a template. Pin the template to the muslin or tulle and cut out.

2 Sew the cupid to one corner of the napkin using tiny running stitches. Do this as neatly as you can, so that the stitches are invisible.

3 Sew three seed-pearl beads to each wing tip of the cupid.

Cross-stitch napkin

For good-looking cross stitch the stitches must be completely regular, so checked or gingham fabric makes an ideal ready-made grid. This very easy project is ideal if you have not done much embroidery before. The bold stitches would also add a hand-made quality to a set of bought table napkins.

MATERIALS

For each napkin:

- **Heavyweight checked cotton fabric, 48cm/19in square**

- **Pins**

- **Needle and tacking (basting) thread**

- **Sewing machine and matching thread**

- **Stranded embroidery cotton (floss) in a bright contrast colour**

Above *Cross stitch*

1 Turn under the raw edge on each edge of the fabric square, then fold over again to make a narrow hem. Pin and tack (baste), turning in the corners neatly.

2 Machine stitch the double hem in place with a matching thread using straight or zigzag stitch.

3 Thread the needle with all six strands of a length of embroidery cotton (floss) double the width of the napkin and knot the end. Leaving a blank row of checks, start at one end of a row with the knot on the wrong side. Stitch diagonally across alternate squares to the end of the row. Finish with a double stitch.

4 Rethread the needle as before, then work back along the same row, crossing over each diagonal stitch. Repeat to make a pattern of three cross-stitch rows at opposite ends of the napkin.

Lemon slice napkin

This lovely bright yellow napkin, embroidered with a succulent lemon slice, would look delightful on a table set for a summer lunch in the garden. If you're embroidering a whole set of napkins you could vary the colours of the stitches to make slices of lime and orange.

MATERIALS

For each napkin:

- **Tracing paper**
- **Soft and hard pencils**
- **Scissors**
- **Pins**
- **Large yellow napkin**
- **Needle and stranded embroidery cotton (floss) in dark and pale yellow, off-white and dark green**

Above *Blanket stitch*

1 Trace the template at the back of the book and draw over the lemon motif on the reverse of the tracing with a soft pencil. Pin the tracing in the corner of the napkin and transfer the motif.

2 Using dark yellow thread, make French knots in the centre of the lemon. Fill the segments in pale yellow stem stitch. Fill the pith in off-white stem stitch, and the skin area with dark yellow French knots. Work dark yellow stem stitch around the edge of the pith and another row outside that in green. Work a dark green running stitch around the French knots and add some small dark green stitches as shading in the segments.

3 Work dark green blanket stitch around the hem of the napkin. The stitches can be worked over the existing machine stitching. Press the embroidery on the reverse side.

Shell-edge napkin

Undyed linen is perfect for table settings with a seashore theme. Buy ready-made napkins or make your own, then trim them with a small shell at each corner, or stitch shells all the way along two opposite sides. The shells will need to have small holes drilled through the tops.

MATERIALS

For each napkin:

- **Undyed linen, about 48cm/19in square**
- **Tape measure**
- **Pins**
- **Sewing machine and matching thread**
- **Needle**
- **Cream cotton perle embroidery thread**
- **16 shells**
- **Length of fine wire**

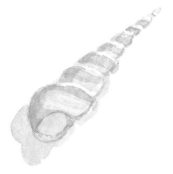

1 Turn in a double hem on all sides of the fabric and press. Mitre the corners and stitch in place. Thread the cotton perle through the shells by first making a large knot at one end of a length of doubled thread. Bend the wire in half and thread the looped end down through the shell. Pass the knotted thread through this.

2 Draw the wire back through the shell, pulling the thread with it. The knotted end should stay securely inside the shell. This process can be a little fiddly, and it works better with some shells than others.

3 Thread the embroidery needle with the unknotted end of the doubled embroidery thread and pass the needle through from the back of the napkin, round the back of the thread at the top of the shell, and through to the back of the napkin to fasten off.

Monograms

Adding a monogram to a napkin is a luxurious touch of ownership. Make them as a wedding gift incorporating the first initial of the Christian names of the couple. Keep the lettering simple and modern or for antique fabrics find an ornate typescript with swirly letters.

MATERIALS

For each napkin:

- **48cm/19in even-weave linen**
- **Stranded embroidery cotton (floss) in one or two colours**
- **Seed beads**
- **Light box**
- **Fabric marker**

1 Make up the napkin following the instructions for Making a Plain Napkin. Arrange the letters of your choice under one corner of the napkin and place both on top of light source. Transfer the letters using the fabric marker pen.

2 To pad the stitching, make short diagonal satin stitches inside the marked lines of the lettering.

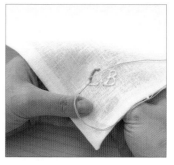

3 Oversew the padding stitches with satin stitch in your choice of colour, this time covering the lines of the letters. Lazy daisy flowers and a scattering of seed beads add pretty decorative details.

Cross-stitch heart

Bold and simple, cross stitch has the naive charm of folk art and is easy to do provided you keep the stitches regular. Here it is used to embroider a heart on a plain napkin.

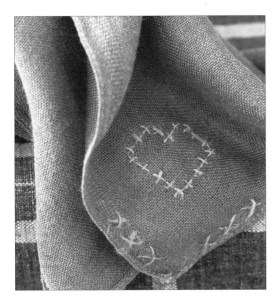

MATERIALS

For each napkin:

• **Pencil, tissue paper and pins**

• **Plain napkin**

• **Needle and stranded embroidery cotton (floss)**

1 Draw a heart in even-sized crosses on a small piece of tissue paper. Pin the paper to the corner of the napkin, then stitch over the crosses.

2 Carefully tear away the tissue paper, leaving the stitched design on the napkin. If any small pieces of paper remain caught under the stitches, use the point of the needle to remove them.

Beaded napkin

This vivid orange linen napkin has been embellished with a row of tiny running stitches in co-ordinating tapestry wool, finished off with a few fine orange beads at each corner.

MATERIALS

For each napkin:

• **Napkin**

• **Orange tapestry wool**

• **Tapestry needle**

• **Scissors**

• **20 small orange beads**

1 Make small running stiches in wool around the napkin border, threading on beads where desired. Here, five evenly spaced beads finish off each corner.

Simple stitching

Used cleverly, embroidery stitches can look highly effective on a plain napkin. Running stitch, French knots and daisy stitch have all been employed here to create a French provincial style.

1 Turn under 1cm/½in around all edges of the chambray and press. Turn under a 4cm/1½in hem and mitre the corners. Slip stitch the hems in place. Press. Using six strands of blue embroidery thread (floss), make large running stitches 2.5cm/1in from the edge all around the napkin. Make another row 5mm/¼in away from the outside edge.

2 Mark the position of the the daisies and French knots. The French knots are positioned in each corner, and then every 10cm/4in, centred between the lines. Using six strands of red thread, make the French knots. Using six strands of blue thread, work daisy stitches between the French knots. Press the napkin on the wrong side.

MATERIALS

For each napkin:

- **Cotton chambray, 60cm/24in square**
- **Tape measure**
- **Needle and matching thread**
- **Blue and red stranded embroidery cotton (floss)**

Ric-rac braid

Grosgrain ribbon teamed with contrasting ric-rac trim gives a smart yet pretty edging to plain napkin. You will need a sewing machine or very neat hand stitching for this project.

MATERIALS

For each napkin:

- **2m/2¼yd grosgrain ribbon 2.5cm/1in wide**
- **Scissors**
- **Pins**
- **Plain napkin, 50cm/20in square**
- **Needle and tacking (basting) thread**
- **Sewing machine**
- **2m/2¼yd ric-rac trim**

1 Cut four 50cm/20in lengths of grosgrain ribbon. Pin along opposite edges of the napkin, turning under the ends. Pin, tack (baste), then stitch all around. Repeat with the remaining two sides.

2 Pin and tack the ric-rac so it overlaps the edge of the ribbon where it meets the napkin. At the corners, manipulate the ric-rac so that it forms a continuous piece. Sew in place, turning the ends in.

Easy embroidery

Simple embroidery can make a very effective edging for a set of napkins, especially if you choose strong colours and make the stitches large for a bold, modern statement. Blanket stitch, oversized oversewing and cross stitch are all easy to do; the knack is to keep the stitches evenly spaced.

MATERIALS

For each napkin:

- **Plain even-weave napkin**
- **Needle**
- **Stranded embroidery cotton (floss) in a toning or contrasting colour**
- **Scissors**

1 Oversewing is easy to do. Simply thread a length of cotton on to a needle and knot one end. With the knot on the wrong side of the napkin make large stitches from the back to the front.

2 Blanket stitch is a well-known favourite stitch that provides a neat edging. Keep the stitches large and use a thick thread so that the work is quickly completed.

3 Cross stitch is one of the quickest stitches to make and can be used to add a hint of contrasting colour to a bright napkin for a truly contemporary feel.

CROSS STITCH

Cross-stitch worked in magenta on a bright orange napkin creates a strong contemporary colourscheme. Choose a ready-made napkin with an even weave and a rough, homespun texture, and use the machine-stitched hem around the edge to guide your embroidery stitches. Work with six strands of embroidery cotton (floss) and make the crosses up to 1cm/¹/₂in wide for a bold effect.

Hand-painted motif

If you don't enjoy sewing you can use paint to decorate plain napkins. There is a large choice of suitable fabric paints and pens, specially designed so that the finished work can be pressed with a hot iron to set the colour. Use paints for bold all-over designs, thick pens for strong lines and fine pens for details.

MATERIALS

For each napkin:

- **Tracing paper**
- **Black felt-tipped pen**
- **Dressmaker's carbon**
- **Plain white napkin**
- **Fabric pens in black and yellow**

1 Trace the bee template at the back of the book using a black felt-tipped pen. Place dressmaker's carbon over the corner of the napkin with the traced design over the top. Draw over the design to transfer it to the fabric.

2 Draw in the traced outline with a black fabric-dye pen, then fill in with a yellow fabric-dye pen. When dry, iron to fix the dye.

Clover leaf tablecloth and napkin

This fresh four-leaf clover pattern is made with a potato print. The cut potato exudes a starchy liquid that blends into the ink and adds translucence. The best fabric to print on is 100 per cent cotton or natural fabric, pre-washed to remove any glaze or stiffener.

MATERIALS

- **Medium-size fresh potato**
- **Sharp knife and cutting board**
- **Small artist's paintbrush**
- **Craft knife**
- **Leaf green water-based block printing fabric ink**
- **Sheet of glass**
- **Palette knife**
- **Small gloss paint roller**
- **White 100 per cent cotton tablecloth and napkins, washed and ironed**
- **Matching thread**
- **Sewing machine**

1 Cut the potato in half in one stroke to give a flat surface. Paint the clover leaf shape on the cut surface of the potato. Cut around the shape using a craft knife.

2 Cut around the internal shapes. Scoop out the potato flesh with the end of the knife blade. Cut away the waste potato to a depth of 6mm/¼in.

3 Squeeze some printing ink on to the sheet of glass and run the roller over it until it is thoroughly coated. Apply an even coating of ink to the potato stamp.

4 Arrange the tablecloth and napkins on a waterproof surface and print the pattern at random. Re-ink the potato after every two printings to vary the intensity of the colour. Leave the finished fabric to dry then press to set the design.

Painted "cross-stitch" napkin

This clever imitation of cross stitch can be achieved quickly and easily with one colour of fabric paint and a fine artist's paintbrush. Instead of sewing the running stitches around the hem you could paint these too if you prefer. To make the project even simpler you could use ready-made napkins.

  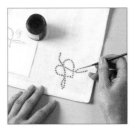 

1 Turn in the raw edges of the linen square and press a 1cm/½in hem. Mitre the corners and press. Tack (baste) the hem and stitch in place.

Trace the heart template provided and the required letters for the monogram.

2 Place the tracing on the corner of the napkin 2.5cm/1in from the edges. Put a piece of dressmaker's carbon paper under the tracing, chalk-side down. Pin. With an embroidery needle, prick through both layers of paper, making closely spaced holes along the lines of the pattern to transfer the image.

3 Mix a heaped tablespoonful of cerise fabric paint with a teaspoonful of fabric medium. Using a fine paintbrush and following the lines of the transfer, paint a series of small crosses to give the illusion of cross stitch. Leave to dry.

4 With a length of stranded embroidery cotton split into three strands, sew a running stitch over the machine stitching around the hem. Using a warm dry iron, press the back of each napkin to set the paint and iron the napkin flat.

MATERIALS

For each napkin:

- **White linen, 52cm/21in square**
- **Scissors**
- **Pins**
- **Needle and tacking (basting) thread**
- **Sewing machine and matching thread**
- **Tracing paper and pencil**
- **Dressmaker's carbon**
- **Large embroidery needle**
- **Cerise fabric paint**
- **Fabric medium**
- **Fine artist's paintbrush**
- **Stranded embroidery cotton (floss) to match paint**

Napkin rings

With imagination and creativity, napkins can be dressed with rings and all kinds of ties fashioned from a wide variety of materials, selected to complement the table setting and inspire your guests. Attention to detail will help to create a special dining environment.

Inspirational ideas

Dress up your napkins with original rings and ties to create table settings with a sense of occasion. The same linens can take on quite different personalities depending on whether they are clasped with a sparkling jewel, trimmed with beads or tied with ribbons and a seasonal flower. Napkin rings can be bought in many styles, or made from wire or natural materials.

Above A diamanté buckle makes a glamorous ring for a pale pink napkin.

Above A curled pipe cleaner is a novel and very simply made napkin ring.

Above White tape trimmed with shells is an inexpensive and easy napkin tie.

Above Twisted twigs threaded with beads look stunning around white linen.

Above A flamboyant cerise bow contrasts beautifully with a purple napkin.

Above An assortment of glass beads on fine wire have a jewel-like appearance.

Above *Single hydrangea florets look delicately pretty on pale green napkins.*

Above *Narrow satin ribbon is simply knotted with a tiny flower sprig tucked in.*

Above *A row of silk daisies looks enchanting around a striped napkin.*

Above *Ordinary piping cord, finger-knitted into a simple chain, perfectly complements blue and white checked cotton.*

Above *This lovely flower is made from brightly coloured beads threaded on wire and is attached to a spiral ring of silver wire.*

Above *Buttoned-up string in pistachio green looks fresh and contemporary.*

Above *Strings of pearly beads look stylish tied around a classic white napkin.*

Above *Lustrous plaited cord gives a Celtic touch to elegant grey linen napkins.*

Orchid napkin tie

The elegant shape of a perfect white orchid head makes a delicate but sophisticated napkin tie – the perfect complement to pure white linen. This exotic flower would look lovely as part of an all-white table setting, with the dark green leaves adding just the right amount of definition to the design.

MATERIALS

For each napkin:

- **25cm/10in narrow off-white ribbon**
- **2 leaves**
- **1 orchid or other similar white flower**

1 Loosely pleat the napkin to fit on the plate. Make a tuck in it if the napkin is too large.

2 Loosely tie the narrow ribbon around the middle of the napkin.

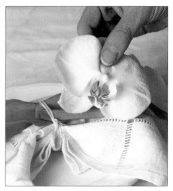

3 Carefully tuck the leaves into the ribbon, then add the flower.

Riveted leaf napkin ring

Any large, leathery leaves can be quickly transformed into napkin rings. These are made from the enormous leaves of *Fatsia japonica*, an evergreen that puts on astounding growth in spring. Riveting them together is both quick and easy, using a small riveting kit available at a haberdashery.

MATERIALS

For each napkin:

- **Fatsia japonica leaf, or similar**
- **Secateurs (pruners)**
- **2 rivets**
- **Riveting pliers**

1 Fold the napkin into a triangle and roll the ends into the middle.

2 Choose a half-grown leaf, as it will retain its bright green shade and be at its most pliable. Cut off the stalk of the leaf you have selected.

3 Wrap the leaf around the napkin. Secure in position by riveting the sides together using riveting pliers.

Scented napkin ring

Inspired by hair "scrunchies", these cardamom-filled organza napkin rings make elegant yet inexpensive table accessories. Cardamom is a perfect spice to use for the filling. With its fresh, sweet perfume it will enhance the ambience of the table without overwhelming the aroma of the food.

MATERIALS

For each napkin ring:

- **Metal-shot organza, 46 x 15cm/18 x 6in**
- **15cm/6in elastic**
- **Needle and matching thread**
- **Bodkin or safety pin**
- **Green cardamom pods**

1 Fold the organza strip in half lengthwise, with right sides together. Stitch a 5mm/¼in seam down the long edge to form a tube. Turn right-side out.

2 Turn in the raw edge at one short end of the organza and tack (baste). Use the bodkin or safety pin to thread the elastic through the organza tube and stitch the two ends of elastic together.

3 Loosely fill the scrunchie with a handful of green cardamom pods.

4 Tuck the raw edge of the organza tube under the basted edge, and slip stitch the two ends of the tube together to enclose the filling. Make sure you match the seams at the join.

Buttoned wrap

Edge and encircle napkins with a beautiful fabric loop and create real chic by securing it with a natural mother-of-pearl button. You need only a small amount of fabric so buy the very best for exquisite results. Make different colours and invidualize a wrap for each member of the family.

MATERIALS

For each napkin ring:

- **Strip of fabric, 10 x 17cm/4 x 6¾in**
- **Pins**
- **Needle and thread**

- **Tape measure**
- **Scissors**
- **Sewing machine**
- **Mother-of-pearl button, 2cm/¾in in diameter**

1 Fold the fabric in half with right sides together to form a strip measuring 5 x 17cm/2 x 6¾in. Pin, tack (baste) and stitch a 5mm/¼in seam down the long edge. Fold the strip in half lengthwise to find the centre of a short edge, and place a pin at this point. At one end, measure 3cm/1¼in from the top down each side of the strip, and place a pin on each side of the strip. Use these pins as markers from which to cut the end to a point, then square off the tip. Stitch a 5mm/¼in seam around the pointed end.

2 Turn right-side out. Turn under 5mm/¼in at the straight end of the strip and slip stitch together. Press. Work a line of machine stitching close to the edge around the whole wrap for a neat finish. Make a machine-stitched buttonhole at the pointed end to fit the mother-of-pearl button and stitch the button in position at the straight end.

Celebrate with paper

Cost effective, cheerful and with an infinite variety of colours and finishes, paper napkin rings can add fun to any party. Browse around art stores for special hand-made paper, but you can achieve original effects with the most everyday materials, such as brown wrapping paper and corrugated cardboard.

MATERIALS

For each napkin ring:

- **Thick paper in dark blue and lime green**
- **Ruler**
- **PVA (white) glue**
- **Craft knife and cutting mat**

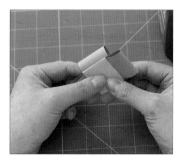

1 Using the ruler as a straightedge, cut two strips of blue paper about 15cm/6in long and 2.5cm/1in wide. Using one strip to form the napkin ring, lap one end over the other and glue.

2 Bring the ends of the second strip to the middle and glue. Tear a short strip of lime green paper and glue it around the centre of the bow. Glue the whole bow to the napkin ring.

OTHER CREATIVE WAYS WITH PAPER

Concertina ring

Crease a sheet of paper concertina-style into 2.5cm/1in widths along its length, then tear it into strips to give slightly rough edges. Punch holes through all the layers. Test the ring for length around a napkin, then thread coloured paper ribbon through the holes and tie.

Layered paper ring

Tear a 15cm/6in strip of paper, 2.5cm/1in wide. Tear a slightly shorter and narrower length of contrasting paper and glue this centrally on top of the first strip. Add a torn paper square in the centre. Once the napkin ring is dry, punch a hole in each end, thread string through and tie to secure.

Paper fan

Fans lend a touch of frivolity to a party table. Simply concertina a small piece of paper, fold in half and glue the centre together to form the fan, then glue the whole ensemble on to a basic paper napkin ring.

Paper star

Crisp and smart, there is something rather lovely about the juxtaposition of pure white paper with traditional starched linen. Paper napkin rings may be throwaway, but with a little imagination and good sharp creases, they can be made to look very special indeed.

MATERIALS

For each napkin ring:

- **Sheet of A4 cartridge paper (29 x 42cm/11½ x 16½in)**
- **Scissors**
- **Strong white thread or fine wire**
- **Double-sided tape**
- **Paper glue (optional)**

Paper lantern

Cut a piece of paper 21 x 15cm/8½ x 6in. Fold it in half lengthwise and make a series of cuts 1cm/½in apart from the folded side of the paper, finishing the cuts about 2.5cm/1in before you reach the edges of the paper. Unfold the paper and bend into a ring. Stick the short edges together to complete the lantern.

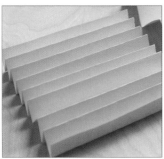

1 Cut a sheet of cartridge paper in half crosswise and fold one half into narrow accordion pleats. Press firmly on each fold to ensure sharp creases. From the remaining paper cut a 2.5cm/1in-wide strip to form the napkin ring.

2 Secure the pleated paper tightly in the centre with a piece of thread or fine wire. Snip diagonally across both ends of the pleats to form points.

3 Fan out the pleated paper to form a complete star. Pinch the two end points together at each side and fold over once to secure the star shape. Join the ends of the paper strip with double-sided tape to form a napkin ring, then tape or glue this to the back of the star.

Foil place tag

Avoid awkward moments when seating guests by giving every setting a place name. Luggage style labels, crafted from foil, are practical, pleasing and give a modern twist to classic white table linen. The silver of the tags complements the tableware perfectly.

MATERIALS

For each tag:

- **2 pieces of modelling foil, each 4 x 6cm/1½ x 2¼ in**
- **Double-sided tape**
- **Embossing tool or empty ballpoint pen**
- **Hole punch**
- **Silver ribbon**
- **Cutting mat**

1 Stick the two pieces of modelling foil together using double-sided tape to make the label more substantial. Trim off the two top corners at 45 degrees to create a traditional luggage-label shape.

2 Emboss the design with your guest's initials or name using an embossing tool or empty ballpoint pen. Punch a hole in the top of the tag and thread the silver ribbon through, then tie around the napkin.

Fine wirework

It is always thrilling when you find a way to transform the most ordinary household items into something quite beautiful. If it is quick and easy, so much the better. These simple ideas using twisted fine wire fall right into that category, and make wonderful napkin holders.

MATERIALS

For each napkin ring:

- **Length of two-core black electrical wire**
- **Wire cutters**
- **Small pliers (optional)**
- **Fine wire**

1 Separate the two-core wire by tearing the strips apart. Cut a length of wire about 15cm/6in long for the body of the dragonfly, fold it in half and twist the two ends together.

2 Make two large loops by wrapping the wire round your hand and twist at the base to form wings. Twist the ends of the wire around the body near the looped end.

3 Bend a length of fine wire into a circle to create a napkin ring. Twist the ends together to join and wrap them around the dragonfly's body. Trim the ends.

OTHER CREATIVE WAYS WITH WIRE

Hovering bee

Turn in one end of a piece of galvanized wire, then wrap the wire a few times around a cylindrical object, such as a rolling pin, depending on how tight you want the spiral to be. Remove the mould, cut the wire leaving an elongated end, and attach an ornament to the end of the wire.

Plaited ring

Divide a length of two-core electrical wire into single strips by tearing it down the middle. Cut a strand into three equal lengths and plait loosely to make a band of the required length. Trim the ends and twist them together to make a ring. Finish by glueing on a silver bead.

A trio of medallions

Divide a length of two-core electrical wire as before and twist it tightly into three small coils. Use a second length of wire to wrap around the coils to secure them, looping them together as you do so. Loop the top coil to a ring of fine wire to hold the napkin.

Fretwork-style felt

Felt doesn't fray, so it can be cut into intricate shapes – and there is no need to hem around fiddly corners. Equipped with the sharpest scissors you can find, there is no end to the designs you can cut.

MATERIALS

For each napkin ring:

- Felt squares in two contrasting colours
- Tape measure
- Sharp embroidery scissors
- Tracing paper and pencil
- Stiff paper or cardboard
- Scissors for paper
- Pins
- Marker pen
- Fabric glue

- Needle and matching thread
- Small button

Star place cards

Draw a star on paper and transfer this to stiff paper or cardboard to use as a pattern. Cut out the star from felt, embroider an initial on it, then glue to a piece of stiff folded cardboard or cartridge paper.

1 Cut a strip 7cm/2¾in wide from each square of coloured felt.

2 To make a template for the appliquéd decoration, trace the template from the back of the book and transfer it on to cardboard or stiff paper. Cut out. Place the template on one of the strips of felt and trace around the pattern using a pen, then cut out the shape carefully, just inside the outline, using very sharp scissors.

3 Using fabric glue, stick the fretwork pattern to the napkin ring or hand-sew it using small running stitches. Turn under and glue a 1cm/½in hem along each long side of the strip to give it a little stiffness. Stitch a small button to one end and cut a hole at the other end the same distance from each side for fastening.

Bead napkin ring

This elaborate-looking ring is easy to make. You need small beads for the sides and large ones for the "rungs", but they don't need to match: a variety of beads makes the finished ring more attractive.

MATERIALS

For each napkin ring:

- Strong beading thread
- Scissors
- 2 long, fine beading needles

- **Large glass beads of approximately the same length, but varying in width and design**
- **Smaller glass beads, in two contrasting colours and slightly different sizes**

1 Cut a length of strong thread and thread a needle on to each end. Position one large bead in the centre of the thread. Add three small beads to each side of the large bead.

2 Add a large bead to one side, then pass the other needle through it in the opposite direction. Pull both threads taut. Thread three small beads on to each needle.

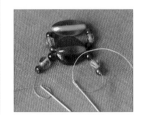

3 Repeat until the chain of beads is long enough to fit comfortably around a napkin. Complete by threading both needle ends back through the first bead. Knot the ends of the thread securely, thread back through a few beads and trim.

Ethnic napkin ring

Interesting beads can be knotted on to a leather thong to make a highly effective napkin ring.

MATERIALS

For each napkin ring:

- **30cm/12in tanned leather thong**
- **Selection of wooden and seed beads**

1 Make a knot about 5cm/2in from one end of the thong. Thread on a few beads of varying sizes, then tie another knot. Tie a third knot a short distance from the second knot. Add a few more beads, then tie another knot.

2 Continue threading on beads until you reach 5cm/2in from the other end of the thong. Tie the final knot. Loop the thong twice around the napkin.

Filigree beading

This delightful, intricate-looking beaded napkin ring is surprisingly robust. Made from glass embroidery beads and threaded on to silvery galvanized wire, it has a sparkle that is reminiscent of diamanté. A set of these sparkling rings would be the perfect accessory for a romantic table setting.

MATERIALS

For each napkin ring:

- **Galvanized wire or beading wire**
- **Scissors or wire cutters**
- **Pliers**
- **Glass embroidery beads**

1 Cut a long length of galvanized or beading wire. Use pliers to bend one end into a small loop to stop the beads from slipping off. Thread the beads on to the whole length of the wire, then bend the other end to secure them.

2 Fashion the beaded wire into a flower shape and secure the "petals" by looping the wire around the centre. With the remaining length of the beaded wire make a ring to go around the napkin and twist the end behind the flower to secure.

OTHER CREATIVE WAYS WITH BEADS

Beaded initial

Thread short lengths of galvanized or beading wire with beads and bend them into curly letters, joining with fine wire where necessary. Tie to a napkin using fine silver cord.

Snowflake

If you don't have the time to thread the beads yourself, look out for shop-bought examples of beadwork, like this snowflake, and thread them on to fine silver cord to tie around napkins.

Punched-metal napkin ring

Modelling aluminium foil, which is available in rolls from specialist art suppliers, is strong yet easy to cut and handle. Here, it is transformed into a smart napkin ring embossed with a heart motif. A strong packaging tube makes a perfect mould for the ring, keeping it in shape while the design is punched.

MATERIALS

For each napkin ring:

- **Strip of modelling aluminium foil, 15 x 6cm/6 x 2½in**
- **Scissors**
- **Packaging tube**
- **Masking tape**
- **Pencil and paper**
- **Pin or bodkin**
- **Silver-coloured adhesive tape**

1 Fold under a 5mm/¼in hem along each long edge of the foil strip then wrap it around a strong packaging tube and secure the ends with masking tape.

2 Prick evenly spaced holes along each edge. Make a paper template for the heart motif and prick holes all round it. Join the ends of the ring with tape.

Silver service

Silvery stainless steel brings a stylish glint to contemporary table settings. This unusual and original napkin ring is a perfect match for the clean lines of modern cutlery, but is made of nothing more sophisticated than a handful of safety pins, cleverly threaded on to shirring elastic.

MATERIALS

For each napkin ring:

- **Shirring elastic**
- **30–40 stainless steel safety pins of uniform size**

1 Tie one end of a length of shirring elastic to the ring at the bottom of one of the safety pins. Thread on the rest of the safety pins. When you get to the end, undo the original knot and tie the ends of the elastic together in a reef knot. Shuffle the pins along to hide the knot.

2 Now repeat the process with a new length of elastic, threading it through the other end of the pins to complete the napkin ring.

A touch of gold

Gold decoration on pure white china makes a glorious combination and lends an air of celebration to any occasion. Use water-based gouache paint, if you prefer to restore the napkin rings to their pure white form after the occasion, or gold ceramic paint for a more permanent, washable result.

MATERIALS

For each napkin ring:

- **2 small white elastic bands**
- **White china napkin ring**
- **Cotton buds (swabs)**
- **Gold gouache or gold ceramic paint**
- **Fine artist's paintbrush (optional)**

1 To create perfect gold circles, put two elastic bands around the napkin ring. Once they are correctly aligned, use a cotton bud (swab) to paint a line of gold spots between them. An easy way to make sure the gold spots are evenly spaced is to use clock positions as a guide. First of all, paint the 12 o'clock position, then 6, then 3, then 9, then fill in with either one or two spots in between.

2 Once the spots are dry, touch in the elastic bands with the gold paint, using another cotton bud (swab) or a very fine artist's paintbrush.

Daisy napkin ring

The stout cardboard tubes that support rolls of furnishing fabric are an ideal size for making napkin rings, and one tube will make dozens of rings. It's possible to use thinner cardboard tubing for these painted rings, but you will need to apply more layers of papier mâché to make them rigid.

MATERIALS

For each napkin ring:

- **Heavy-duty cardboard tube**
- **Hacksaw**
- **Scissors**
- **Newspaper**
- **PVA (white) glue**
- **Mixing bowl**
- **Fine sandpaper**
- **White emulsion (latex) paint**
- **Paintbrush**
- **Water-soluble coloured pencils**
- **Gold marker pen**
- **Acrylic spray varnish**

1 Using a hacksaw, cut a 5cm/2in section of tube. Trim and tidy the edges if necessary, using scissors.

2 Tear a sheet of newspaper into narrow strips and soak in diluted PVA (white) glue. Cover the rings inside and out in two layers of papier-mâché. Leave to dry.

3 Rub the surface and edges down lightly with fine sandpaper, then paint with two coats of white emulsion (latex) paint, leaving it to dry between coats. Decorate with water-soluble coloured pencils, and edge with a gold marker pen.

4 Spray the napkin ring inside and out with a coat of acrylic varnish. Leave to dry.

The art of napkin folding

Beautiful starched linen or damask napkins folded into sculptural shapes immediately transform even the simplest table setting into one worthy of the most special occasion. Most napkin folds are easy to accomplish because they are designed to be made and repeated at speed, although a few offer more challenging designs. For the best results when making complex folds, starch all napkins and press each fold in place.

Inspirational ideas

The elegant symmetry of traditional napkin folds is most apparent when they are executed using plain linen napkins. The quality of good linen is shown to its best advantage and the crisp folds, tucks and pleats are beautifully defined in pure white fabric. Coloured napkins can be used to give a more contemporary look or to fit in with a particular theme or occasion.

Above *The understated Cable contrasts well with an elaborately decorated table.*

Above *The Cockscomb is a flamboyant and impressive design.*

Above *The symmetry of the Double Jabot is ideal for very formal tables.*

Above *Chevrons, a neat and simple design, shows off exquisite hemming.*

Above *The simple profile of the Clown's Hat looks effective in large numbers.*

Above *The French Lily is a classic fold with heraldic roots, perfect for a formal table.*

Above *The Lovers' Knot has a modern look when a coloured napkin is used.*

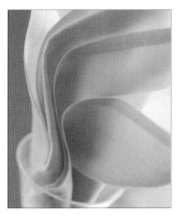

Above *The Flame is a sophisticated design, spectacular in a plain setting.*

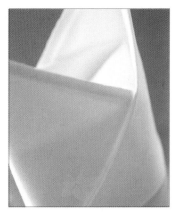

Above *The classic Mitre is the stately king of traditional napkin folds.*

Above *The Wave is an understated, smart design that looks contemporary and is easy to achieve with precision.*

Above *The Diamond is a complex and impressive fold, equally suited to traditional or contemporary table settings.*

Above *The Opera House is a modern design with a witty flourish.*

Above *The Fan is a traditional fold that has a charming simplicity.*

Above *The Carousel is complicated to fold but is a very effective design.*

Easy folds for any time

These neat, elegant folds will bring a little elegance to your table without going over the top. Any one of them would make a thoughtful finishing touch on a table set for a festive family lunch or dinner with friends. It's a good idea to master some of these simple designs before moving on to the more complicated folds later in the book.

Diagonal roll

Rolling fabric is easy, but to keep the roll looking pristine you need to use plenty of starch so that the napkin keeps its crispness. This simple roll is a good choice for a small napkin in fine cotton organdie, which will make a slim shape. A diagonal approach gives an interesting finished outline.

1 With the napkin opened out, right side down and pressed flat, begin rolling it up tightly from one corner. Stop just before you reach the halfway point and hold the roll steady.

2 Turn the napkin and roll up the other half to match the first side.

3 Slide a napkin ring over the rolled napkin and position it as desired on the dinner plate.

Folded roll

This is an easy design to master and make consistent for a whole set of napkins, and it works well using either fabric or soft, thick paper napkins. Begin with a well-pressed napkin and match the corners carefully when making the initial fold. Have a napkin ring to hand to hold the roll in place.

1 Fold the napkin in half diagonally to make a triangle, matching the corners.

2 Roll the napkin tightly, beginning at the longest side of the triangle.

3 Carefully fold the roll in half and secure it with a napkin ring.

Candy cane

For this simple but effective design you will need two fabric or paper napkins of the same size but in different colours. Try using one plain and one patterned napkin, or two strongly contrasting shades.

1 Open the two contrasting napkins and arrange them with right sides down, slightly offset and with the top one higher, so that about 2.5cm/1in of the edge of the lower napkin is visible.

2 Starting with the visible corner of the lower napkin and holding the two napkins together, roll them up tightly, keeping the roll horizontal.

3 As you continue to roll the napkins into a long thin cylinder, the colours and patterns of both will create a striped effect on the outside.

4 Carefully bend the roll in half at the centre, pinching a crease to keep the roll set in a V-shape when laid on the plate or table.

Double scroll

This minimal, tailored design would suit a Japanese-style table setting. You could if you wish position the napkin horizontally on the plate and stand a place card between the two rolls.

1 Press the napkin flat and, with the right side down, fold in two edges to meet in the centre. Press the folds carefully.

2 Roll the napkin up neatly from one short edge, making sure the folded edges stay flat. Stop rolling when you reach the halfway point.

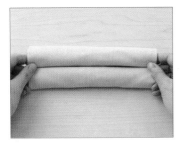

3 Turn the napkin round and roll up the other side. Check that the two rolls match exactly. Hold both rolls at each end to move the napkin to the table.

Night light

Use a fabric napkin for this design – there is too much folding for a paper napkin and it might tear. The napkin doesn't need starching.

1 Open out the napkin and arrange it as a diamond. Fold it in half from bottom to top to create a large triangle. Fold down both layers so that the top corner of the triangle comes to the centre point of the long folded edge.

2 Fold down the top 3cm/1¼in of the short top edge of the napkin. Repeat, folding the napkin evenly until the last fold meets the long edge.

3 Turn up the left-hand end of the folded strip. This end will represent the flame of the night light.

4 Beginning at the turned-up end, roll up the folded strip tightly. When you reach the end, tuck it into the roll at the base of the night light to hide it and secure the roll. Arrange the protruding end so that it resembles a flame.

Scroll

This rolled design makes a small, compact shape, which will sit neatly on a side plate. It is a good way to arrange soft, loosely woven napkins that are not suitable for more sculptural forms.

1 Open out a large napkin and press it flat. Fold the bottom third up, then fold the top third down over the first fold.

2 Turn up a narrow hem on the top layer. Fold this over twice to make a band across the centre of the napkin.

3 Turn the napkin over so the hem is underneath, and roll it up tightly from one short end.

Gathered pleats

This simple unstructured design using a napkin ring looks pretty as part of an informal table setting.
Use it for napkins that have a decorative border, as it creates a feminine, frilled effect.

1 With the napkin opened out and the right side uppermost, take hold of the centre and lift it towards you.

2 Allow random soft pleats to form as the edges of the napkin fall, and grasp it loosely around the middle.

3 Slide a napkin ring over the gathers to hold them in place and spread out the folds to form an attractive shape.

Paper heart

This understated design is perfect for a paper napkin, though it works equally well with fabric, bringing a light-hearted touch of romance to the table for an anniversary, Valentine's day, or just for fun.

1 Open out the paper napkin so that it is double, with the long folded edge nearest you. Pick up the bottom right-hand corner and bring it across the napkin, folding from the centre of the lower edge so that the two sides of the folded section are at equal angles. Press in place.

2 Now bring the bottom left-hand corner up and over the first fold, again folding from the centre point. Align the edge of this fold with the edge below it.

Ice cream cone

Use a plain white or coloured linen napkin for this elegant fold so that its clean geometric lines can be clearly seen.

1 Fold the napkin into quarters with the second fold at the lower right-hand side. Fold the two top layers down to meet the bottom corner.

2 Turn the napkin over. Fold the left side two thirds of the way over the napkin.

3 Fold the right-hand edge in over the previous fold to align with the edge.

4 Tuck the corner of the upper section over the fold beneath it to secure.

Geometric style

Eye-catching and elegantly precise, this contemporary design calls for napkins with a crisp finish in a plain colour or a simple pattern, and is well suited to informal entertaining.

1 Fold the napkin diagonally across the centre, with wrong sides together, to form a triangle.

2 Fold the sloping sides down from the top point so that they lie vertically together along the centre line.

3 Fold the two sloping edges into the centre again from the top point so that they meet at the centre line.

4 Turn the napkin over and fold it in half. Tuck the long point into the horizontal fold and turn back again.

Fanned pleats

This is a quick and easy design for the beginner, ideal for a small napkin with interesting decorative detailing. For a more slender shape, you can fold the left-hand edge in under the three pleats.

1 Arrange the napkin diagonally, right side down, and take the bottom corner to the top to make a triangle.

2 Folding from the centre point of the long edge, take the left-hand point across to the right, offsetting it slightly so that it lies about 2.5cm/1in above the lower point.

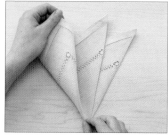

3 Bring the remaining (centre) point of the napkin over in a similar fashion to make the third pleat.

The flag

The triangular shape and multiple points of this asymmetrical design recall a series of fluttering pennants. The underlying straight edge is slightly rolled to represent a flagpole.

1 Fold the napkin in half from top to bottom. Pick up the top layer of the bottom left corner and take it across to the right-hand corner.

2 Turn the napkin over and repeat on the other side to form a triangle. Fold the whole thing in half from right to left.

3 Arrange the four points of the folds so that they are evenly staggered.

4 Roll the vertical edge under the napkin and twist slightly to create the flagpole.

Envelope fold

Eminently elegant, this fold can be accomplished in a trice and is ideal when you are in a hurry but want to make an impression. It looks smartest in pure linen, which falls naturally into soft folds.

1 Fold the napkin in half to form a large rectangle. Next, form a point at one end of the rectangle by folding down each corner toward the centre. This creates the flap of the envelope.

2 Fold the other end of the rectangle over to cover the pointed end. Fold down the corners of this top layer so that it forms a second point lying over the top of the first one.

3 Fold the top point over so that it lies just over the straight folded edge. Crease the fold with your thumb. Bring the second flap over the first and arrange it so that it lies slightly further back than the first, with both points visible.

Breeze

This seemingly artless arrangement gives the impression that a gentle movement of air has caught the layers of the napkin and casually flipped them over, like a breeze riffling the pages of a book.

1 Fold the napkin into quarters, with the second fold at the bottom and the four corners at the top right of the square.

2 Fold the napkin in half again, taking all the layers of the right-hand vertical edge across to the left.

3 ◁ Holding the edges together at the bottom left, take the uppermost corner and peel the top layer over to the right, without flattening the fold.

4 ▷ Repeat with the three remaining layers, making each fold a little shallower to create a layered effect.

Starfish

When you want to add a little height to your table design, but are pushed for time, use the starfish, a chic triangular fold with a well-spread base that allows it to stand up. The starfish is a stylish, unfussy design that looks great when repeated down the length of a long, thin table.

1 Fold the napkin in half diagonally to make a large triangle with the long folded edge at the bottom. Holding the centre point of the lower edge, fold the two sharp points up to the top, so that the edges meet in the centre.

2 Turn the napkin over, keeping it the same way up, and fold the closed point at the bottom to meet the open points at the top.

3 Fold the right-hand half of the triangle over to the left along the centre line.

4 Rotate so that the open edges are at the bottom, and allow the points to spread out to make the standing shape stable.

The wave

Smart yet simple to do, the wave has a tailored look that gives the table an elegant finish. It is an excellent choice when you are entertaining a large party of guests as it is quick to fold and easy to make consistent. Crease the folds very lightly to retain the curves of the wave-like layers.

1 Fold the top third of the napkin down and the bottom third up over it.

2 Fold in a short hem at each end of the rectangle.

3 Fold the left-hand edge across to the right, stopping a little short of the edge to leave a border.

4 Take the new left-hand edge across, leaving a similar border, to create a layered effect.

Knotted napkin

Tying a knot seems one of the easiest ways to arrange a napkin, but making each knot look elegant may take a bit of practice. This style works best with an unstarched napkin made of a soft fabric.

1 If you are using a large napkin, turn in two opposite corners a few times to make the fabric more manageable.

2 Grasp the two turned-in edges and pinch them gently together in the centre.

3 Keeping hold of the centre of the napkin, form a loose knot with the two ends.

4 Pull the ends gently so that the knot has some shape but is not tight.

Wings

This light-hearted design works best with a stiff cotton napkin and is quick to capture the imagination of guests, particularly of young children, as it resembles a butterfly settled on a plate.

1 Fold the upper and lower edges to the centre, then take the lower edge to the top, folding in half lengthwise.

2 Fold the right-hand edge a third of the way to the left.

3 Double this edge back to the right, creating a pleat. Repeat the last two folds on the left side.

4 Push the lower corners of the upper layers inwards. The thickness of the fabric should lift the "wings" slightly.

Sailing boat

This jolly arrangement is perfect for a waterside meal, but even if you are not within sight of the sea you can bring out the marine theme by decorating the table with related pieces such as shells and pebbles.

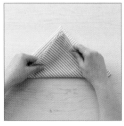

1 Fold the napkin into quarters with the open corners nearest you. Fold them up to the top point.

2 Fold the sloping sides downward from the top point so that the outer edges meet in the centre.

3 Turn the napkin over, keeping it the same way up, and fold up the lower section. Fold the triangular shape now formed vertically along the centre.

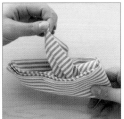

4 Hold with the open edges uppermost. Carefully tease out one of the loose points from the tapered end of the boat, to form the "sail".

Pure and simple

As its name suggests, this design is quickly arranged and pleasing to the eye. The result focuses attention on one corner, so it is particularly effective for napkins with a lace trim or embroidered motif.

1 Open out the napkin and arrange it diagonally, with right side down. If there is a motif in one corner place this at the top. Take the bottom corner to the top and press the fold to make a large triangle. Holding the centre of the bottom fold, take the sharp left-hand point up to meet the top corner of the napkin.

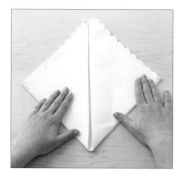

2 Repeat with the other side so that the edges meet in the centre.

3 ◁ Take the left side of the diamond and fold it in from the bottom so that the edge aligns with the centre. Repeat on the other side to make a kite shape.

4 ▷ Turn the napkin over. Turn up the bottom point and press in place.

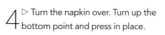

Cockscomb

This is an impressive fold that is very effective for small, intimate occasions. A few of these flamboyant cockscombs on the table transform the simplest setting into something special.

1 Fold the napkin into quarters, and arrange it so that the open corners are at the bottom, nearest you.

2 Take the four open corners up to the top, folding the napkin into a triangle.

3 Holding the top corner, fold the right-hand sloping edge downward to lie along the vertical centre line.

4 Repeat on the other side to make a kite shape, making sure the sides and corners meet accurately.

5 Fold the two triangular tabs at the bottom up at the back of the large triangle.

6 Keeping hold of the tabs at the back, bend the sides of the triangle back, folding vertically along the centre line.

7 Arrange the napkin horizontally with all the individual layers lying along the upper edge.

8 Holding the lower edge firmly in one hand, use the other to tease out the layers one at a time, arranging them with a similar space between each.

Pure elegance

This dignified design is equally suitable for formal occasions and low-key meals. Its triangular shape and broad base makes it very stable and it is easy to construct.

1 Open out the napkin with right side down. Fold the bottom edge up by a third and fold the top third down over it. Fold in the short sides of the resulting rectangle to meet in the centre.

2 Fold the upper corners diagonally down to the centre line.

3 Turn the napkin over from side to side, keeping the point at the top.

4 Turn in each end of the long side and tuck one end into the pocket in the other; this forms the back of the design. Turn the napkin over and stand it up.

Duck step

Though it is really a very abstract shape, the duck step is appropriately named. It is a basic napkin fold that is geometrically pleasing and easy to construct but gives a satisfyingly three-dimensional result.

1 Fold the napkin in half bottom to top, then fold the lower edge to the top once more.

2 Holding the centre top point, fold the right-hand upper edge down to lie along the centre line.

3 Repeat with the remaining side so that the edges meet. Turn the napkin over, keeping the point at the top.

4 Lift the top section so that it stands upright. Fold it back slightly so that the "feet" splay and it stays standing.

Lover's knot

A neat twist on every plate looks elegant and modern in a contemporary setting. This very orderly knot is a tidy way to arrange large napkins, and looks especially good when executed using brightly coloured plain napkins, which allow its symmetry and sharp contours to speak for themselves.

1 Open the napkin with right side down and fold it in half, taking the bottom up to the top edge. Press the crease.

2 Double the napkin over lengthwise once more to establish the central crease. Open out this second fold again.

3 Turn up the bottom folded edge to align with the creased centre line.

4 Fold down the open edges at the top to meet the folded edge in the centre.

5 Fold in half again lengthwise, folding from top to bottom to give a neat finish on the outer edges of the knot.

6 Fold down the right-hand half so that the folded edge is vertical, half the width of the strip away from the centre.

7 Fold the left half of the strip down from the same point on the top edge, folding it back (this end will appear longer).

8 Fold the longer end of the strip back a second time, swinging it to the front to lie on top of the right-hand section.

Clown's hat

Tall clowns' hats look wonderful standing on plates along the length of a dinner table. Their unfussy silhouette works well when multiplied. Alternate napkins in two different tones to create a light and shade effect with these distinctive shapes.

1 Fold the napkin in half top to bottom, then fold the top right-hand corner down so that the edges align at the bottom of the napkin.

2 Fold the right-hand triangle over to the left along the centre line, again aligning the lower edges.

3 Bring the upper left-hand corner over to the lower right. Holding the side, place your hand inside to open the "cone".

4 Carefully turn the lower edges out to create a "brim" around the hat. This also locks the folds together and creates a stable shape that will stand up.

Diamond

The diamond is not ostentatious but is seriously chic and will add flair to the smartest of tables. Using very few folds it cleverly creates a small square set diagonally on top of a larger one.

1 Fold down the top third of the napkin, then fold the bottom third over it. Fold in the two left-hand corners to meet each other, as if making a paper plane.

2 Fold the right-hand portion of the strip down at 45 degrees, aligning the upper edge with the edges of the two small triangular flaps.

3 ◁ Fold the top section over at 45 degrees to the right-hand corner. This will create the small diamond for the top.

4 ▷ Fold the remainder of the napkin underneath, so that the crease runs under the lowest corner of the diamond.

Fans and pleats

Once you have mastered some of the classic simple shapes you may want to try your hand at more ornate pleated and layered designs. Any one of these would create a stir at your table. Precise folding is vital to achieving a perfect finish, so some simple calculations may be needed before you begin, to guarantee beautifully even pleats.

Mathematics for concertina pleats

For many of the pleated designs in this book you may simply "concertina-pleat" the napkin randomly from bottom to top in a familiar "fan" style, folding the lower edge over to create a horizontal border, then doubling the material back and forth upon itself. However, for a more accurately folded design, you may prefer to use the following mathematical method, which is much-used in origami. The principles are illustrated here using a square of paper, but the same method can be applied to napkins, whether paper or fabric, and whether the pleats are arranged diagonally or horizontally. The process involves folding and unfolding several horizontal creases, depending on how many divisions you need to make.

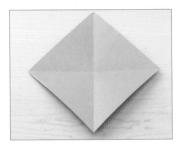

1 Fold and unfold the square diagonally in half both ways to find the centre.

2 Fold the lower corner to the centre, then unfold.

3 Repeat with the upper corner. The resulting creases divide the square horizontally into four equal sections.

4 Fold and unfold the upper and lower corners to the first horizontal crease.

5 Take the lower corner and fold it across the centre line to the quarter line at the upper end of the diamond. Repeat with the upper corner.

6 The unfolded diamond will be creased horizontally into eighths.

7 ◁ Turn the paper over keeping the eighths creases horizontal. Fold and unfold upper and lower corners to the eighths.

8 ▷ Continue this process logically until you have divided the square into sixteenths.

Napkin ring

You can apply the method of folding equal divisions shown opposite to create a wonderful napkin ring. Use it to hold an elegant rolled napkin or to secure one of the designs in this book.

1 Divide the square of paper diagonally into sixteenths and make the concertina folds from one corner into the centre.

2 Repeat the folds on the remaining half of the paper. Note that the central diagonal remains unfolded, so the final strip is two sixteenths wide.

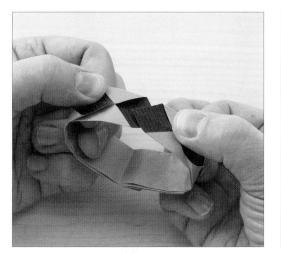

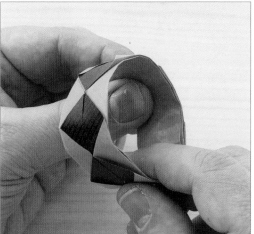

3 Carefully flatten all the creases, then turn the strip over and roll it around your hand into a ring, tucking one end into the folds created by the pleating at the other end. The outside should appear as a succession of alternate diamonds and triangles.

4 Carefully shape the ring. The tension and curve of the paper will ensure that the design stays together.

Bishop's hat

This is a traditional method of folding large dinner napkins, and stands very securely. The proportions are important, so it may be necessary to adjust the spacing of some of the folds to suit your particular napkins as you work through the steps.

1 Arrange the napkin diagonally and fold it almost in half, taking the bottom corner not quite to the top but leaving a slender border around the upper edge.

2 Fold the lower corners toward the top, leaving a small space between them.

3 Fold the bottom corner up, again taking it not quite to the top corner.

4 Fold the same corner back down, leaving a border at the bottom of the napkin. Turn the napkin over and roll into a cylinder, tucking the corner at one end into the pocket at the other.

Festival

The billowing, flame-like pleats of this bold fan design make it an ideal choice for colourful napkins and lively occasions. Use firmly woven fabric that will hold the pleats, but keep the creases soft.

1 Arrange the open napkin as a diamond and fold the top corner down to meet the point nearest you. Fold down a pleat along the long edge.

2 Make concertina pleats all the way to the corner, keeping the pleats even. Flatten them with your hand but do not press them.

3 Fold the pleated napkin in half so that the two ends of the long edge meet. Pinch at the base to hold the shape and arrange on the table, allowing the pleats to fan out a little.

Iris in a glass

This design creates a very striking display if folded using large, colourful napkins. Arranged in a row of elegant stemmed wine glasses, the folded napkins resemble stately garden flowers.

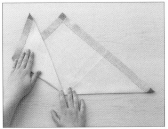

1 Arrange the open napkin in a diamond shape right side down and fold the bottom corner up to the top, matching the hems. Holding the centre point of the long lower edge, fold the two sharp points upward at an angle, leaving an equal space between each point and the central corner. Press the folds.

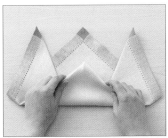

2 Fold the lower corner to the halfway point and turn the napkin 90 degrees.

3 Concertina-pleat vertically across the folded napkin, making about six pleats. Place the pleated napkin in the glass and shape the "petals".

Spiral ribbon

Looking like a twirling Spanish dancer, this unusual design is full of movement. Use a starched napkin that will hold the shape well. The final shaping of the top section is tricky and takes practice.

1 Arrange the open napkin in a square and concertina-pleat it into sixteenths, starting at the lower edge.

2 Tightly roll the strip to approximately two thirds of the way along, then stand the roll upright on the table, making sure the unrolled section of the napkin is right side up.

3 ◁ Allow the unrolled material to fan out, guiding it round to form the "skirt".

4 ▷ Holding the coil, turn the napkin over and tuck the loose end into one of the pleats. Turn the napkin back and take hold of the corner at the centre of the coil; very carefully tease it upward and outward to form the "body" of the figure.

Palm leaf

Napkin rings don't have to sit around the middle of napkins. In this arrangement a chunky ring acts as a container for a dramatic large leaf design. An extra fold at the base helps to support the folds, but a sturdy starched napkin is required to maintain the vertical pleats.

1 Fold the napkin diagonally, with the folded edge nearest you.

2 Fold the right-hand corner upward at a slight angle, starting a little away from the centre. Repeat on the other side.

3 Fold the lower edge upward to create a slender band at the base.

4 Make six vertical concertina pleats in the napkin. Slide into a napkin ring and allow the top portion to fall open naturally.

Morning sun

Ideal for a weekend breakfast, this small fan represents the rays of the rising sun. An unpleated section at the back acts as a support to keep the pleats together and helps the folded napkin to stand up.

1 Fold the bottom third of the napkin up and then fold the top third down over the first fold.

2 Turn the napkin 90 degrees and make eight even concertina pleats from one short end, leaving the final 5cm/2in of the strip unfolded.

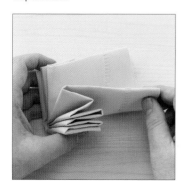

3 ◁ Turn the napkin over and fold it in half so that the pleats are on the outside.

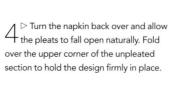

4 ▷ Turn the napkin back over and allow the pleats to fall open naturally. Fold over the upper corner of the unpleated section to hold the design firmly in place.

Double fan

This classic design is ideal for formal dinners. It is satisfying to accomplish but needs a little time to practise it. You will need large starched cotton napkins for the best effect.

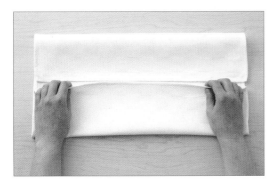

1 With the open napkin horizontal and right side down, begin by folding both upper and lower edges to the centre.

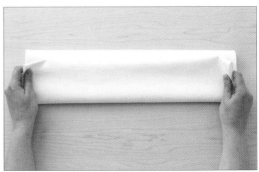

2 Fold the napkin in half again by bringing the bottom folded edge up to meet the top.

3 Rotate the napkin so it is arranged vertically. Make eight even concertina pleats.

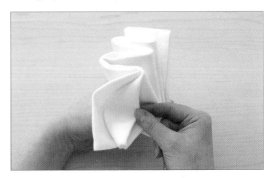

4 Make sure the double edge is at the top. Holding the fan together at the bottom with one hand, pull down the single edge inside each pleat to make triangular inversions.

5 Fold down the loose corners at each end to align with the folded edges behind.

6 Turn the napkin around and repeat step 4 on the other side, again folding down the edge inside each pleat.

7 When all the folds have been made the triangular "tucks" on each side should be staggered, creating a zigzag effect.

8 Allow the pleats to open at the top so that the ends fall to the table, keeping the bottom tightly pinched together.

Fanned bow

The fanned bow is perfect for festive occasions, especially if you use a highly decorative napkin ring or a sparkling ribbon tie to secure the centre. The circular shape is perfect on large dinner plates.

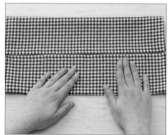

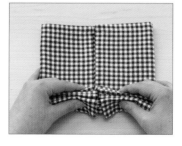

1 Arrange the napkin horizontally, right side down, and fold in the upper and lower edges to meet at the centre.

2 Rotate the napkin so that the short end of the rectangle is nearest you, and fold it into 12 even concertina pleats. Press the pleats firmly.

3 Secure the centre of the napkin with narrow ribbon or push a napkin ring into the centre. Fan out the pleats to make a circular shape.

Spreading fan

This elegant, simple design is suitable for all occasions. It is a very pretty way to arrange a napkin with a decorative hem, as the pleats draw attention to a continuous design such as cutwork or embroidery.

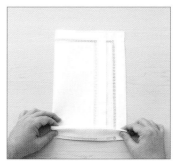

1 Arrange the napkin square, right side down, and fold the left-hand side over to the right so that the hemmed edge finishes a little short of the other side. This means both hems will be visible.

2 Make even concertina pleats in the napkin from bottom to top.

3 Clasping the fan together at the centre, slip a napkin ring or a similar fastener around the lower half of the pleats to secure in place.

Springtime

For this rather complex design you will need a large fabric napkin that will hold a crease. A contrasting border or decorative hem will add definition to the tumbling shapes of the pleats.

1 Fold the napkin in half horizontally, with the fold at the bottom. Lift the nearer edge of the top layer and make concertina pleats all the way to the fold.

2 Grasp the pleats firmly and turn the napkin over with the pleats nearest you. Holding the centre point, fold up the two sides so that the edges of the pleats meet vertically in the centre.

3 Carefully turn the napkin over again from top to bottom.

4 Fold the bottom right and left corners up to the top point, tucking them into the pocket created by the pleats.

5 Fold the napkin in half, bringing the top point down to the bottom.

6 Fold the top point away from you again, so that it extends only slightly beyond the top edge.

7 Fold each side corner in toward the centre, and tuck one inside the other.

8 Turn the napkin over carefully and fan out the pleats to create the final shape.

Parasol

Both plain and patterned napkins are appropriate for this attractive design. You will also need a napkin ring or a short length of contrasting ribbon for each napkin to hold the pleats in place.

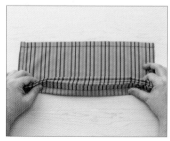

1 With the napkin open and right side up, make concertina pleats from the bottom edge to the top, folding the napkin into sixteenths.

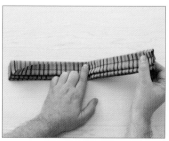

2 Holding a finger firmly at the centre carefully fold the pleated napkin in half from side to side.

3 Slide a napkin ring half way up the pleats and then fan out the top to make the parasol.

Knotted ribbon

The central knot of this design can be quite bulky because of the number of concertina folds, so use napkins in a fine, crisp fabric about 35cm/14in square. Paper is not really suitable as it may tear.

1 Press the napkin flat and lay it out square. Beginning at the edge nearest to you, pleat the napkin horizontally into sixteenths, pinch-pressing each fold as you make it.

2 Holding the napkin tightly to keep the pleats together, carefully tie the central part into a single knot.

3 ◁ Pull the knot closed but leave it fairly loose so that a guest can undo it easily to use the napkin. It will take some practice to ensure that the finished knot is perfectly central.

4 ▷ Pull out the ends of the pleats into a fan shape.

The fan

Use a carefully starched linen napkin for this classic fold, which can be used for any kind of occasion. It is cleverly designed so that it sits upright securely without any support.

1 Press the napkin flat and lay square, right side down. Fold it horizontally from bottom to top.

2 Fold the left side over to the right to fold the napkin into quarters.

3 Unfold step 2, and align the left-hand edge with the central crease you have just made. Make a firm crease.

4 Pull the vertical edge at the centre back across to the right, so that the napkin is again folded in quarters.

5 Take hold of the sharp crease made in step 3, slide it back towards the left and lay it over the left-hand edge, thus creating a pleat.

6 Fold the same edge back to the left, aligning it with the left-hand edge, making a further pleat.

7 Turn the napkin over bottom to top, keeping the pleated portion on the left, and carefully fold it in half horizontally, so that the pleats appear on the outside.

8 Fold the upper edges of the unpleated right-hand portion down at 45 degrees so that the edges align with the pleats.

9 Fold the excess material at the base (a small rectangle) back underneath the triangular section. This helps to stabilize the form of the finished design.

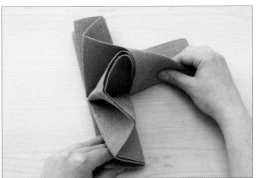

10 Lift the triangular section until it stands upright from the remaining material. The fan will also rise to a vertical position. Allow the pleats to splay apart naturally.

Fire

This is a spectacular fold that does justice to any special occasion. Using napkins in orange or red it lives up to its name and makes a striking choice for a dinner party, while in pure white or cream the fold takes on a sophisticated flower-like look, perfect for a wedding.

1 Begin with the napkin folded into quarters, arranged as a diamond with the four free corners at the bottom.

2 Fold the upper two layers of the napkin up, matching the corners to the top point of the diamond.

3 Turn the napkin over and repeat with the other two layers on the reverse side to form a triangle.

4 Fold the right-hand half of the triangle across to the left.

5 Fold the same point back to the right by a third of its length, so that one third protrudes beyond the centre fold.

6 Now fold the same point back to the left again, so the upper section is pleated into thirds.

7 Turn the napkin over, keeping it the same way up, and repeat the lateral folds with the triangle on the reverse side.

8 Tightly holding the lower half, tease and spread the points at the top to create the flames. Arrange the napkin in a glass.

Double jabot

The stately double jabot makes an elegant statement on the smartest of tables, but for all its sophistication it is not difficult to do, so it is a viable option for folding in quantity for large formal occasions. Stunning in white double damask, this fold also looks good in strong colours.

1 Fold the napkin into quarters, and arrange as a square with the open corners at the top right.

2 Fold the top layer of fabric diagonally from top right to bottom left, aligning the hems with the folded edges.

3 Fold this triangular flap back on itself by one quarter of its length, parallel with the first diagonal fold.

4 Make two further concertina pleats in the top layer, so that the corner of the napkin finishes at the centre.

5 Rotate the napkin and repeat the concertina folds in the opposite direction with the second layer.

6 Fold the napkin in half along a diagonal from bottom left to top right, keeping the zigzag pattern on the outside.

7 Bring the two sharp points together and tuck one inside the other. Turn the napkin around to place on the table.

Diamond breeze

This charming informal napkin fold is great for displaying impeccably stitched hems, and combines crisp corners and sculptural lines with a softly draped effect.

1 Press the napkin flat then fold into quarters, with right side out, and arrange in a diamond shape with the open corners at the bottom.

2 Fold the napkin in half diagonally from top to bottom to form a triangle.

3 Turn back the top layer, making the fold close to the long bottom edge of the triangle. Repeat with the second layer, placing it a little further back.

4 Repeat with the remaining layers, keeping the spacing between the hems even and the folds soft.

Scallop

This layered arrangement is given an interesting three-dimensional quality by creating a small tuck at the top that supports the scalloped edges. It looks delicate and pretty in white damask.

1 Fold the napkin into quarters and arrange in a diamond with the four open corners at the top. Fold down the first layer leaving a slender border along the lower edges.

2 Repeat with the three other layers, leaving equal spaces between the hems.

3 Holding the centre point of the upper edge, fold the left side down so that the top edge lies along the vertical centre line. Fold down the right side to match it.

4 Fold back the top point to about halfway down the centre line. Holding it under the napkin, open out the side flaps in soft curves to create scalloped edges.

Chevrons

Made with neatly hemmed and crisply starched plain linen napkins, this design stands with military precision. It adds height to the table and looks smartest with plain, modern china and glassware.

1 Begin with the napkin folded into quarters and with all the open corners at the bottom.

2 Fold the single layer at the bottom up toward the top, leaving a slender border along the upper edges.

3 Fold the second layer up, leaving a border around the edge of the same width as for the first layer.

4 Fold up the third corner, again creating an equal border around the hemmed edges.

5 Repeat with the last layer. Turn the napkin over keeping it the same way up and holding all the layers in place.

6 Roll the triangle around your hand into a cylinder, tucking the corner from one side into one of the folds on the other side.

7 Check the alignment of all the layers, then turn the napkin around to stand on the table.

Cream horn

This shape works well with any type of napkin, but for the best effect use it for those with a fairly loose weave and a soft feel. It makes a compact shape suitable for placing on small plates.

1 Begin with the napkin folded into quarters and arranged in a diamond with the four open corners at the bottom. Pick up the first layer and fold it back so that the hemmed edge sits below the upper folded edges.

2 Repeat with the next two layers, leaving equal spaces between the hems.

3 Turn up just a small amount of the final layer so that the lower edge is quite short. Holding all the layers in place, turn the napkin over, keeping the open corners pointing away from you.

4 Holding the centre of the lower edge, curl the sides in so that they meet in the centre. Turn the napkin over to arrange on the plate.

Spear

Though small and neat, this spearhead design makes a strong statement. It shows off the beautiful texture of crisp linen and its sharp angles look best in a minimalist, contemporary setting. It's important to make sure the hems are accurately spaced as attention is focused on them.

1 Fold the napkin into quarters and arrange in a diamond with the open corners at the bottom. Fold back one layer, aligning it with the upper edge.

2 Fold back the remaining layers, staggering the hems evenly.

3 Carefully turn the napkin over from top to bottom. Fold in the sides so that the folded edges meet vertically in the centre.

Flowerbud

This charming upstanding design has a fresh, graceful appearance, suitable for a summer lunch party. It is an ideal design for good-quality paper napkins as well as patterned or figured fabric.

1 Fold the napkin in half diagonally, right side out, and fold the top corner down to the bottom to create a triangle.

2 From the centre of the long edge, fold the left-hand sharp point down to the right-angled corner and repeat with the right-hand side so that the edges meet vertically in the centre.

3 Fold the bottom half of the resulting diamond shape up to the top to make a triangle.

4 Fold the two uppermost layers down toward you, so that about half the point protrudes below the lower edge.

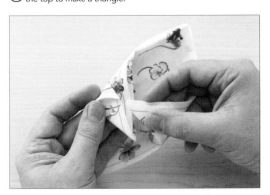

5 Turn the napkin over and roll into a cylinder around your hand, tucking one sharp corner into the pocket of the other.

6 Turn the napkin around and tuck the lower flap up inside the cylinder to help hold the folds in place.

7 Holding the lower section, pull down the two loose points from the top to form "petals".

8 Shape the "bud" at the centre by opening out the front slit and rounding the sides to give the desired effect.

Tulip

Chunky linen napkins with an interesting texture will give substance to this lovely simple design. It is easier to manipulate the folds to give a shapely result when using soft, pliable fabric.

1 Begin by folding the napkin in half diagonally, folding the bottom corner up to the top.

2 Fold both layers of the top corner down so that they touch the centre of the lower edge.

3 From the centre of the lower edge, fold the right-hand side across at an angle of about 30 degrees from the vertical.

4 Repeat with the left-hand side, so that the two sections overlap with the sharp points at the same height.

5 Holding the previous folds, turn the napkin over from top to bottom.

6 Fold up the two lower points, pulling them apart slightly.

7 Shape the bloom by folding the outer edges back at the desired angle.

Cicada

This innovative design is ideal for printed paper napkins, as its effectiveness is enhanced by the unprinted wrong side appearing as a panel across the centre of the insect.

1 Arrange the open napkin, right side down, as a diamond and fold the bottom half over the top to form a triangle.

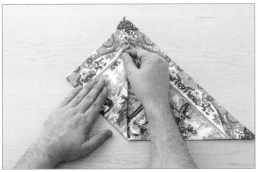

2 From the centre of the long bottom edge, fold the sharp corners at left and right up to the right-angled top corner.

3 Fold these corners back down at a slight angle, creating a space between the central point and each of the "wings".

4 Fold down the single layer so that the corner comes just above the central point. The wrong side will be visible.

5 Fold down the remaining layer to a higher point, creating a V-shaped panel across the body.

6 Turn the napkin over and fold the sides inward at an angle to shape the body. Turn the napkin over to place on the table.

French lily

A charming traditional fold, the French lily is reminiscent of the heraldic fleur-de-lys, with its historic associations. Choose large, starched napkins for this one, as they help to keep the lily in shape.

1 Arrange the napkin in a diamond and fold the bottom corner up to the top corner to form a triangle.

2 Fold the two sharp points up to the right-angled corner so that the folded edges meet vertically in the centre.

3 Turn up the lower corner to approximately three quarters of the way up the middle of the napkin.

4 Turn the upper part of the previous fold back down toward you so that the point touches the lower edge.

5 Turn the napkin over and roll it into a cylinder around your hand, overlapping the two outer corners.

6 Tuck one end into the pocket formed by the folds in the other end, to hold the napkin together.

7 Turn the napkin around and curl down the loose flaps at either side, tucking the points inside the lower pocket.

Napkins for
special events

Festive meals, children's celebrations and family

birthdays and anniversaries all deserve their own special

table settings, and this section contains some really

novel and creative napkin designs to amuse and delight

guests of all ages.

Heart

A heart on a plate conveys an unmistakable romantic message for an intimate dinner. This is an easy shape to make but needs to be folded with precision and requires napkins that will hold creases well, so choose crisp linen – in pink or red, of course.

1 Fold the napkin in half, bringing the top edge down to meet the bottom edge. Fold almost in half again, bringing the bottom edge up just short of the top.

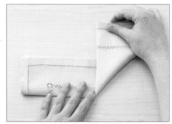

2 Holding the centre point of the bottom edge of the napkin, fold the right-hand side up vertically.

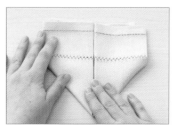

3 Repeat with the left side, creating a sharp point at the base of the heart.

4 Shape the top of the heart by folding the four top corners underneath.

The knot

This is a very simple, unstructured design, but you can load it with symbolism when it's used to decorate the table for a romantic candlelit dinner, or an anniversary breakfast. It takes a little practice and a confident hand to make a casual-looking yet stylish shape.

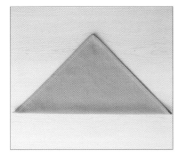

1 Arrange the open napkin in the form of a diamond, with right side down, and fold the bottom point up to the top to make a triangle.

2 Starting from the long edge, make concertina pleats up to the point.

3 With the pleats facing away from you, fold the right point over the left and tuck back through the loop created to form a loose but tidy knot.

Valentine rose

In this wonderful flight of fancy, an ordinary paper napkin turns into a very realistic-looking rose. It's unlikely that you or your guest will want to dismantle it, so provide more napkins for the meal.

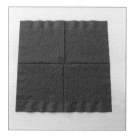

1 Begin with the napkin opened out completely and arranged as a square.

2 Fold over the left-hand vertical edge to create a border. Many paper napkins have a perforated design that can act as a guide.

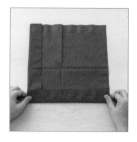

3 Fold up the lower edge to make a matching border along the bottom.

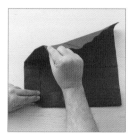

4 Place two fingers at the lower left corner, pointing inward, and grasp this corner. Take hold of the top of the napkin with your right hand.

5 Wrap the napkin over and around your fingers, with the aiming of creating a neat cylindrical roll.

6 Once you have a slender tube, pinch it together about 5cm/2in from the top; the top part will form the bud.

7 Roll the stem tightly from the bud down, taking care not to tear the paper. Stop halfway down.

8 Take hold of the loose corner at the base of the stem and start teasing it up toward the bud.

9 Gradually pull out the excess paper a little at a time, straightening the stem as necessary before continuing.

10 The corner of the flap will become the leaf. Below it, continue twisting the stem tightly to the bottom, then shape the leaf.

11 For a fuller bloom with more inner petals, take hold of the corner of the paper in the middle of the bud and twist to tighten the spiral.

12 Curl the upper edges of the petals, creating a very fine border, to define the form of the flower when viewed from the side.

Easter bunny

These perky bunny ears are the perfect greeting for young partygoers arriving at the table – and they're especially appropriate at Easter. The brighter the napkins you choose for this design, the better.

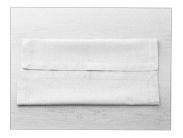

1 Fold both the upper and lower edges of the napkin to the centre.

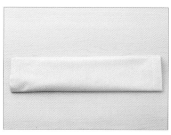

2 Fold the napkin in half by bringing the bottom edge up to the top edge.

3 Fold the right-hand side of the napkin up from the centre point so that the folded edge is vertical.

4 Fold both layers of the top right-hand corner diagonally down to the centre.

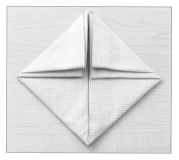

5 Repeat the last two steps on the left-hand side to form a diamond shape.

6 Fold the right-hand upper edge down to the vertical centre line and repeat with the left-hand upper edge.

7 Holding the folds in place, fold the bottom point up underneath, forming a triangle.

8 Take the bottom corner on one side across and tuck it into the pocket on the other side to form the base. Round out the shape of the base from underneath using your finger.

9 Turn the napkin round and shape the head by opening out and rounding the small "pouch" beneath the ears.

Coronet

A stately crown in starched white damask at each place setting looks dignified for a formal occasion, but you could also use this design in rich festive colours to complete a Christmas table.

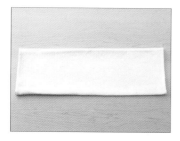

1 Arrange the open napkin as a square, right side down, and fold it horizontally into thirds.

2 Fold each short edge in to lie a short distance from the centre, leaving a gap.

3 Fold the bottom left and top right corners in at 45 degrees so that the edges meet along the vertical centre line.

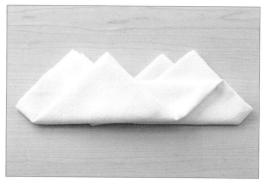

4 Turn the napkin over and rotate it so that a diagonal edge is at the bottom. Fold the upper edge down to the lower edge, allowing the loose corners to flip out.

5 All four points should now be positioned at the top. Tuck the right-hand point between the two diagonals at the left-hand side.

6 Turn the napkin over and repeat, tucking the other end into the fold behind the front triangle.

7 Shape the design by carefully opening out the base to separate the two sides and rounding out the top.

The swan

Although the swan can be made from stiff fabric, thin paper napkins work better. If you wish, you can slide the chest of the swan between the prongs of an upturned fork, which can then be placed across the plate to hold the napkin in place. The design is free-standing, however.

1 Keeping the napkin folded into quarters, arrange it as a diamond with an open corner at the top. Fold it in half vertically to establish the vertical diagonal, then unfold it.

2 Fold the right-hand corner to the vertical centre line and repeat on the left to form a kite shape.

3 Turn the napkin over keeping the sharp point nearest you and the open corners at the top. Fold in the left-hand outer edge to the centre, holding the napkin firmly to stop the layers unfolding.

4 Fold in the right-hand outer edge to the vertical centre line to match the previous fold.

5 Fold the napkin in half, taking the sharp point at the bottom up to the top.

6 Fold approximately one third of the sharp point back down toward you to create the head of the swan.

7 Fold the napkin in half lengthwise, bending the sides back. The neck and head flaps should finish on the outside.

8 Hold the napkin firmly along the lower edge of the body with one hand.

9 Lift the neck away from the body and flatten the base to keep it in place. Lift and flatten the head. Gently pull up the layers to form the body of the swan.

The corsage

For this attractive flower-like design a small and a large napkin are folded as one. This would be a nice arrangement for a meal in which paper napkins are needed for a first course eaten with the fingers.

1 Place a small napkin on top of a larger one, so that there is a border of equal width all round the edge. Arrange as a diamond.

2 Carefully fold both napkins in half diagonally as one, right sides together, with the smaller of the two napkins on the inside.

3 Fold the napkin carefully into quarters.

4 Lift the top triangle to a vertical position and allow it to open out symmetrically, rotating the napkin so the open edges are nearest you.

5 Begin squashing the upper folded edge down, and flatten the section to form a diamond shape.

6 Turn the napkin over and repeat the last two steps on the reverse side.

7 Beginning at the closed corner, turn in the folded edge of the top layer, aligning it with the centre line.

8 Repeat on the other side of the top layer, then turn the napkin over and repeat on the other side.

9 Fold the sharp point over at right angles to the central line to touch the edges of the triangular flaps created in steps 7 and 8.

10 Fold the napkin tightly in half along its length. Turn the napkin over. Holding the closed end firmly with one hand, start to tease out the four corners.

11 Spread out the four petals to shape the flower and reveal the inner napkin at the centre.

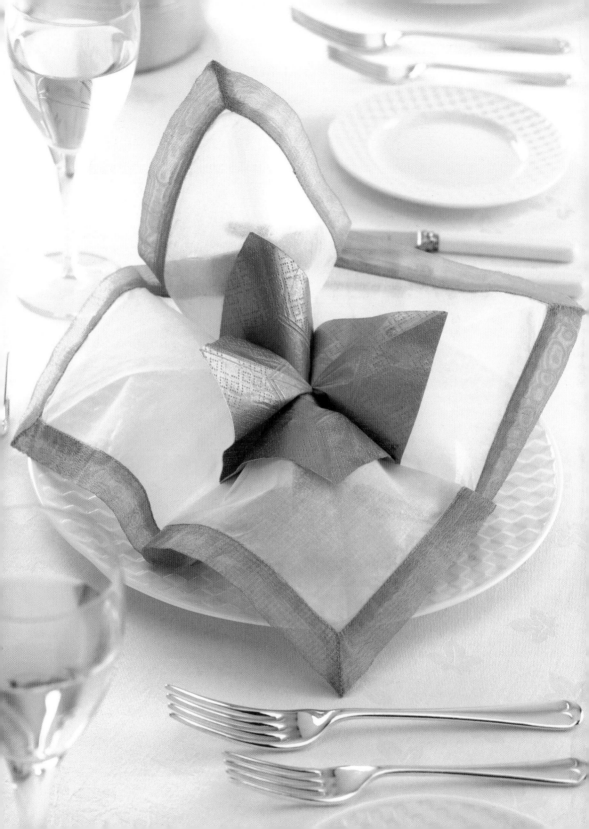

Candle fan

This neat, symmetrically pleated and rolled arrangement is designed to be inserted in a glass and calls for stiffly starched fabric napkins with a fine, firm weave that will hold the creases well, or thick paper.

1 Press the napkin flat and arrange it in a square, right side down. Fold in the left and right outer edges to meet vertically at the centre.

2 Find the centre point and peel back the lower left-hand flap as far as it will comfortably go, making the crease from the centre to the bottom left-hand corner.

3 Repeat with the remaining three corners, so that the two sides of the napkin meet at the centre point only.

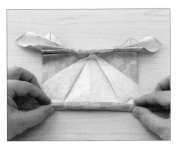

4 Starting at the bottom edge, make six or eight concertina pleats to the horizontal centre line.

5 Use a paperclip to keep this pleated section together while you are working on the remaining half of the napkin.

6 Rotate the napkin by 180 degrees and form the candles by rolling the lower edge up to the centre.

7 Remove the paperclip from the pleated side, and with the rolled section on top, carefully fold the napkin in half lengthwise, bringing the two ends of the roll together.

8 Push the folded centre of the napkin into a glass, allowing the rolls to splay apart a little and the pleats to open to produce the desired shape.

Butterfly

This pleated design looks pretty made with delicately coloured and patterned paper napkins, creating a collection of butterflies to settle lightly on your table for a summer lunch party.

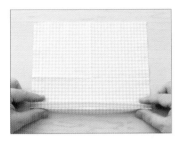

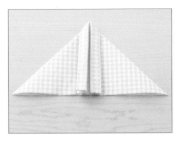

1 Arrange the napkin in a square and make concertina pleats from the bottom edge, dividing the lower half into eighths. The centre line of the napkin should be used to form the final pleat.

2 Turn the napkin over so that the pleated portion lies underneath at the top, and the shape is a rectangle. Fold the top right-hand corner down at 45 degrees so that the edges of the pleats align with the central vertical line.

3 Fold the top left-hand corner down at 45 degrees to match the other side and form a triangle.

4 Turn the napkin over from side to side and fold the top point down to the lower edge.

5 Fold this point back up again so that its tip (the head of the butterfly) protrudes above the body.

6 Fold the right-hand sharp point up so that the lower edge lies along the vertical centre line.

7 Fold this triangle back down so that the point touches the lower edge.

8 Fold the right-hand half of the napkin, including all the layers, across to the left along the central vertical line.

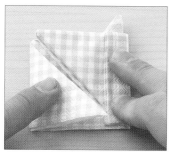

9 Fold the left-hand corner to the centre, aligning the lower edges.

10 Fold this small triangular section upward and tuck it into the pocket created in what was the right-hand side.

11 Turn the napkin over and spread the wings. The design is supported by the triangular section under the body.

The duck

An inventive design to appeal to cartoon fans of all ages, this impressionistic version of the hot-tempered Donald Duck glowers up from under his rakishly tilted peaked cap.

1 Press the napkin flat and arrange in a diamond. Fold it in half diagonally, taking the bottom corner to the top, to make a triangle.

2 Fold up a slender border along the lower edge of the triangle.

3 Find the centre of the lower edge and fold up the left-hand side a little away from that point. Repeat with the right-hand side so the points meet at the top.

4 Fold the lower edge approximately three quarters of the way up the vertical centre line.

5 Double this short edge back down to the bottom of the napkin, creating a pleat, as shown.

6 Turn the napkin over and roll into a cylinder, tucking one side into the diagonal folds created in the other side.

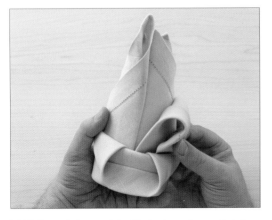

7 Curl over the loose points at the top to create eyes; tuck the ends inside the pleated section below to secure.

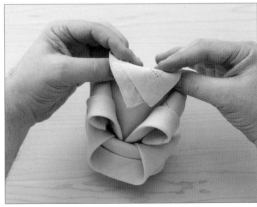

8 Fold the top points over and shape to suggest the duck's peaked cap.

Turbo

Designed to stand in a tall glass and very easy and quick to do, this napkin is meant to loosely represent a space rocket, so it would be a good choice for a child's birthday party table. Use paper napkins with bold, brightly coloured motifs.

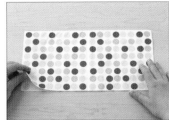

1 Fold the napkin in half with the fold along the top edge.

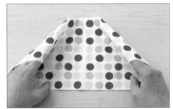

2 Hold one of the top corners tightly in each hand and carefully roll the napkin in from each corner over your fingers.

3 As the rolls get closer to the centre you may need to turn the napkin in your hands so that you don't let go of it.

4 Try to keep the two rolls even. When you reach the centre, place the napkin point down in a glass to hold the shape.

The dog

This is an ideal design for small children, and would work well with either fabric or paper napkins. A few small candies are used to make the eyes and nose as a winning finishing touch.

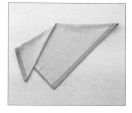

1 Arrange the napkin as a diamond with right side down. Fold the top half down, aligning the edges, to make a triangle. Find the centre of the long edge, and from that point fold the left-hand side down at about 30 degrees.

2 Fold the right-hand side down at the same angle to form the ears. Turn under about one third of the folds along each sloping side.

3 Turn under the top point of the napkin to form the top of the dog's head.

4 Turn up both layers of the bottom corners to form the dog's snout. Arrange a candy nose centrally at the top of this flap and add the two eyes.

GI cap

Always popular with children, this little hat will inevitably start off on the heads of young guests rather than in their laps. It looks best in crisp linen in deep colours such as navy or green.

1 With the napkin arranged as a square, right side down, fold the top edge down to the bottom edge, then fold in the left and right edges of the rectangle to meet in the centre.

2 Take hold of the inner loose corner of the right-hand portion and peel open the single layer of material to the right, while holding the second layer in place. As you do this allow the upper section to flatten into a triangle. Repeat with the top layer of fabric on the left.

3 ◁ Turn the napkin over and fold in both outer edges to the centre.

4 ▷ Fold the single layer at the bottom up to the horizontal centre line, then double this portion over again. Turn the napkin over and repeat on the remaining side. Open out the napkin so that it stands freely with the folded edge along the top. Use your thumb to dimple this edge.

Flame

Make this uncomplicated shape using beautifully textured and hemmed linen napkins in rich, deep tones to add a series of stately vertical forms to a sophisticated table setting.

1 Begin by folding the napkin into quarters, right side out, and arrange as a diamond with the open corners nearest you at the bottom.

2 Fold a single layer from the bottom corner upward, leaving a slender border along the upper edges.

3 ◁ Repeat with the remaining layers of the napkin, staggering the edges equally beneath the preceding layers.

4 ▷ Turn the napkin over and roll it into a cylinder, tucking the corner of one side in between the layers of the other.

Samurai helmet

The traditional origami design for a model of a Japanese warrior's helmet translates very effectively into a fold for fabric or paper napkins, creating a pleasingly detailed symmetrical form.

1 Arrange the open napkin as a diamond and fold it in half diagonally, taking the top corner to the bottom.

2 From the centre of the long top edge, fold each of the sharp points of the triangle down to the right-angled corner, forming a diamond.

3 Fold the two sharp points back up to the top corner.

4 Fold each sharp point outward so that the folded edge is at right angles to the long sloping edge, to form the "wings".

5 Pick up a single layer at the lower corner and fold it upward so that the point is about halfway up the upper triangle.

6 Double over the portion of this layer below the central horizontal fold to create a "brim" across the base.

7 Turn the napkin over and fold the remaining layer at the lower edge all the way up behind to form the back of the helmet.

Mr spoon

This ingenious design has a spoon slotted into its folds, which forms the head of a little man lying in each plate ready to join in the fun of a party meal. It will delight children and grown-ups alike.

1 Open out the napkin and arrange as a square, with right side down. Fold in the upper and lower edges so that they meet at the horizontal centre line.

2 Find the centre point and open out each of the four corners diagonally from that point.

3 Beginning with the left-hand side, carefully roll the napkin up to the vertical centre line.

4 Roll up the right side to match. (You may want to pin the first roll in place while working on the other side.)

5 Fold back the upper section of the rolls to form the arms of the little man.

6 Turn the napkin over, and carefully pull the arms apart (this is easier with a fabric napkin) to give the desired effect.

7 Slide the handle of a spoon down inside the layers of the body leaving the bowl protruding to form the head.

Ocean liner

A fleet of these sturdy-looking little ships in brightly coloured paper napkins would be just right for a summer party with a nautical theme, or even for a celebratory picnic at the seaside.

1 Leave the paper napkin folded in quarters and arrange in a diamond with the open corners at the bottom. Fold in half diagonally, bringing the top of the napkin down over the bottom.

2 Rotate the napkin so that the right-angled corner is at the bottom left, then fold up the lower edge to form the hull, making the fold deeper towards the right-hand side.

3 Open out the lower fold and turn the open layers of the hull out and up the other side to enfold the remaining triangular portion of the napkin.

4 Fold the upper triangle down parallel with the hull, then fold it back up and down again once more.

5 Fold the point of the triangle up again. These random pleats will form the cabin and the funnel of the ship.

6 Unfold the concertina pleats made in steps 4 and 5. Open out the diagonal crease of the large triangular portion.

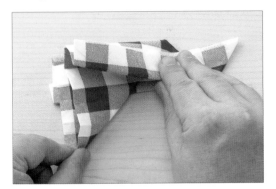

7 Using the creases made in steps 4 and 5, fold the upper corner down and up along the central diagonal.

8 Fold the tip of the upper corner over toward the front of the ship and double it over again to make the funnel.

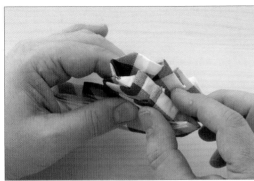

9 At the open back end of the ship turn in a short vertical fold on each side through all the layers.

10 Interlock the pleats in the open ends. Open out the underside of the hull a little so that the ship stands up.

Fish

A streamlined fish with gracefully folded fins and tail is an appropriate idea for a party table with a seaside feel. A single candy eye transforms an almost abstract fold into a creature with personality.

1 Arrange the open napkin in a square, right side up. Fold over the left-hand edge to make a narrow border.

2 Fold the napkin in half horizontally so that the fold at the left-hand side is on the outside.

3 Pick up the top right-hand corner and fold it down at 45 degrees so that the right-hand side of the napkin aligns with the lower edge. Crease then open the fold.

4 Pick up the top layer at the right-hand side, forming the diagonal crease with the layers below. Refold the top layer.

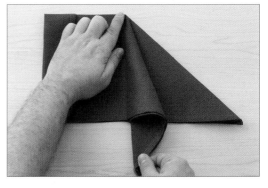

5 Pick up the top layer of the triangular section and fold it under from the top so that the folded edge is vertical.

6 Fold the lower layer to match the previous fold, turning it in the opposite direction.

7 Fold the bottom layer upward, aligning the crease with the tip of the fish's head to form the tail fin.

8 Rotate the napkin slightly so the fish is horizontal and fold up the lower section of the top layer of the body.

9 Fold up the lower section at a shallower angle to complete the fin. Lay the fish on a plate and position the eye.

Christmas tree

This classic fold for a traditional Christmas table is very simple and quick to do but has a satisfying three-dimensional quality, suggesting not only a stylized Christmas tree but also a four-pointed star.

1 Fold the napkin in quarters and arrange it as a square with the open corners at the bottom. Fold in half, bringing the top edge down to the bottom edge.

2 Take hold of the top layer by the lower right-hand corner and slide it over to the lower left corner, allowing the napkin to flatten into a triangular shape. With a paper napkin the vertical centre crease will help this procedure.

3 Turn the napkin over from side to side, keeping it the same way up, and repeat step 2 on the reverse side, creating a triangle.

4 Fold the triangle in half from side to side to create the inner vertical creases, then spread out the branches of the tree vertically and stand up on the table.

Christmas candle

A festive fold based on a universal seasonal symbol is perfect for Christmas. Green or red napkins would be particularly suitable, and a decorative border creates a stylish diagonal accent.

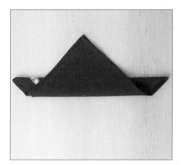

1 Arrange the open napkin as a diamond, right side down, and fold the bottom corner up to the top. Fold the lower edge up to form a narrow border, then turn the napkin over.

2 Rotate the napkin through 90 degrees so that the long folded edge is on the left. Roll up the napkin, beginning from the bottom point and stopping short of the small top tail.

3 ◁ Turn the candle round so that the tail is facing you and tuck it into the band around the base to secure the roll.

4 ▷ Tuck the free corner at the top down into the roll and form a flame shape with the second free corner underneath.

Christmas stocking

This jolly Christmas stocking will add some festive cheer to your party table – you could even hide a little extra gift inside, or arrange a candy cane sticking out of the top to complete the picture.

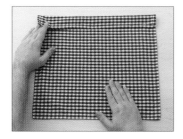

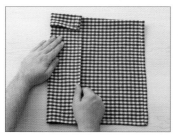

1 Arrange the napkin in a square, right side down, and fold over a narrow border along the upper edge.

2 Turn the napkin over from side to side so that the folded border lies under the upper edge. Fold the two sides in so that the edges meet along the vertical centre line.

3 Fold the two lower corners in at 45 degrees, aligning the sides along the vertical centre line.

4 Fold up the point at the bottom of the napkin so that it meets the centre of the long edge of the triangular section.

5 Holding the lower folds in place, fold the napkin in half from bottom to top.

6 Fold down the upper layer toward you, lining up the corner of the triangle with the right-angle beneath, to create a pleat.

7 Fold the napkin in half vertically. Holding the top section, swing out the excess fabric in the pleat to angle the toe.

Christmas star

This elegant six-pointed star is satisfying to fold and makes a simple statement on an elaborately decorated Christmas table. The flat, symmetrical shape is a perfect fit for circular dinner plates.

1 Arrange the napkin in a square, right side down, and fold it in half, taking the bottom edge to the top.

2 Open out the napkin again, and take the lower right-hand corner to the left, folding from the top right-hand corner, so that it rests on the centre crease.

3 Fold the bottom edge up at the point where the lower right-hand corner and the two upper corners form an equilateral triangle. (This requires experimentation.)

4 Fold the lower left-hand corner across to form the equilateral triangle described in step 3.

5 Fold the top left-hand corner across to the centre of the right-hand side.

6 Fold this point back outward to form a pleat, aligning the crease with the centre of the napkin.

7 Repeat step 6 with the two remaining corners of the triangle to create the six points of the star.

8 To lock the flaps in place, lift up the corner of the last fold and tuck it under the folded edges of its neighbour. Turn over.

Complex folds

Most traditional napkin designs are swift to fold and simple to remember so that you can use them frequently and consistently. The ideas in this section are mostly representational and are a little more elaborate in construction, but one of these could be just what you need for a themed celebration.

The slipper

Winsome fairytale slippers lend a magical touch to a celebration table. Each napkin makes one slipper, but a pair placed on each plate could make the setting even more appealing. A tiny stick-on gem adds a witty finishing touch to this charming napkin fold.

1 Fold the napkin in half, bringing the top edge down to the bottom.

2 Fold the napkin in half again, bringing the top edge down to the bottom.

3 Fold down the right-hand side at 45 degrees to lie along the vertical centre line.

4 Fold down the left-hand side in the same way so that the folded edges meet.

5 Narrow the point at the top by folding the sloping side in to lie along the vertical centre line.

6 Fold in the remaining side of the napkin to match.

7 Fold the napkin in half along the vertical centre line and hold the napkin so that the folded edge lies along the top. The smooth pointed triangle will become the toe.

8 Rotate the napkin so that it is horizontal. Fold a single layer of the large flap at the rear upward to lie along the edge of the toe section.

9 Fold the excess triangular flap of the underlying layer forward over the edge as shown, to narrow the portion protruding at the heel.

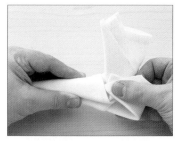

10 Carefully wrap the excess material around and tuck deep inside the pocket created by the edges of the toe section (the shortest edge of the triangle).

11 Stand the napkin upright, flattening the toe to help this, and shape the vertical section by rounding into a kind of cylinder from above.

Water lily

Using a well-starched napkin, this classic design creates a cup shape that can be used to hold a bread roll or a small gift, a few chocolate hearts for Valentine's Day or a tiny posy of spring flowers.

1 Open out the napkin right side down and fold all four corners to the centre.

2 Fold all four corners of the new square you have created to the centre again.

3 Turn the napkin over, using a hand on either side to keep the flaps in place.

4 Pick up each corner of the new square in turn and fold them into the centre once more.

5 Take hold of the loose double flap under one corner and pull it upward so that the point almost turns inside out; you will need to hold down the rest of the napkin firmly with the other hand in the centre. Repeat with the three other corners.

6 Still holding the centre, tease out from underneath the single loose flap between two of the main petals.

7 Repeat with the remaining flaps to create extra petals or leaves all round the water lily.

Mitre

This classic design epitomizes the art of napkin folding. Smart and majestic, it is best reserved for the most formal of occasions. Despite its grandness, however, it is quite quick to fold.

1 Arrange the open napkin as a square, right side down, and fold it in half, bringing the upper edge to meet the lower edge.

2 Fold the top right-hand corner down at 45 degrees to the lower edge, then fold the bottom left-hand corner upward so that the edges meet along the centre line, creating a parallelogram.

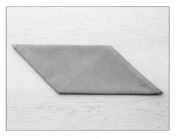

3 Holding the folds in place, turn the napkin over and rotate it so that a diagonal edge is at the bottom.

4 Fold the upper edge down to the lower edge, leaving the loose corner beneath unfolded.

5 Pull out the trapped corner of the front triangular section so that both points are at the top.

6 Fold the right-hand side across on a vertical crease down from the right-hand point.

7 Lift up the large triangular front flap and tuck the loose corner from the previous step behind it.

8 Turn the napkin over and repeat, tucking the other end into the fold behind the front triangle.

9 Shape the napkin by carefully opening out the base to separate the two sides and rounding out the centre.

Carousel

Use crisply starched medium-sized napkins for this spectacular design, which produces a three-dimensional sculptural shape with a circular outline that sits perfectly on a dinner plate.

1 Begin with the napkin folded into quarters, with the open corners at the lower left-hand side.

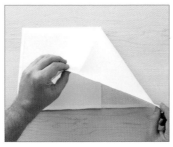

2 Lift up the top layer at the left corner and slide it all the way across to the right, so that the upper folded edge opens and falls over the vertical central line.

3 Turn the napkin over from side to side so that it is still the same way up.

4 Lift up the single layer at the right corner and slide it across to the lower left, again allowing the fabric to flatten.

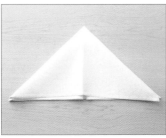

5 Press the folds on the sloping sides, creating a triangle with the open edges at the base.

6 Lift up the single top layer and fold it upward so that the two corners of the napkin are drawn into the centre.

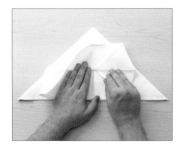

7 You will need to experiment slightly with the position of the fold; the two side corners when flattened should meet in the centre without overlapping.

8 Turn the napkin over and fold up the single layer on the second side to match the first, bringing the other two corners to meet in the centre.

9 Using the vertical centre line as the axis, fold a single layer from the right-hand side across to the left.

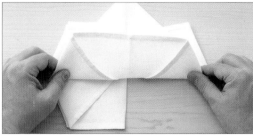

10 Fold the lower edge upward, matching the previous folds. Turn the napkin over once more from side to side and repeat steps 8 and 9 on the other side.

11 Stand the napkin upright and fan out the four main flaps to point north, south, east and west, while allowing the inner folds to fall forward to complete the circular outline.

Nautilus shell

This is an ambitious-looking asymmetical design but the shape is mainly created by folding triangles of diminishing size to achieve the spiral effect. Once you have mastered the technique it is quick to do.

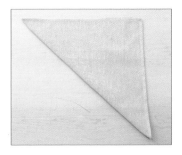

1 Arrange the open napkin as a square, right side down, and fold the lower left corner to the top right to make a triangle.

2 Fold down the top edge so that the two triangles formed on the left and lower right are equal in size.

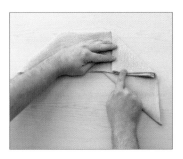

3 Turn in the top right-hand corner at 45 degrees so that the side edge aligns with the edge of the previous fold.

4 Turn in the right-hand side vertically so that it aligns with the edge of the previous fold.

5 Turn in the downward-facing section at 45 degrees, starting the crease in line with the long horizontal edge. Repeat the triangular folds until the end of the section is pointing up.

6 Secure the spiral by tucking the end of the tail section into the previous folds.

7 Pick up the sharp left-hand corner and take it across between the layers of the left-hand section, aligning the bottom edges.

8 Turn in the two triangular sections below the central horizontal line to form the mouth of the shell.

Overcoat

This charming little coat is best made from a paper napkin with a contrasting border design, which will accentuate the clever details such as the sleeves and the stylish narrow lapels. Everyone will love it.

1 Open out the napkin flat. Fold the two vertical edges in to meet at the centre.

2 Turn the napkin over. Turn in a small hem on the same two vertical folds. Press and open out.

3 Turn the napkin over. Find the centre point along the raw edges. Keeping your finger on this point, turn back a small collar at each side.

4 Fold back and press the top third of the napkin.

5 To form the waist, make a pleat so that the folded edge is a third of the way from the bottom edge of the napkin.

6 Open out the top fold, but keep the lower pleat in place.

7 Refold the vertical folds at each side of the napkin.

8 Now refold the napkin one third of the way from the top edge.

9 The back edge of the top fold is used to form the sleeves. Tease out the fold at the sides to form arms.

10 To form the shoulders, turn under a small diagonal fold at each top edge.

Pinwheel

This lovely design looks great on a party table, creating a real sense of movement, and will especially appeal to children as it really does look as if it could turn in the breeze.

1 Open the napkin out flat with right side down, and fold the four corners into the centre to form a diamond.

2 Fold two opposite edges inward to meet in the centre, creating a rectangle.

3 Fold the two short edges of the rectangle to meet in the centre, creating a small square.

4 Carefully tease out the loose corners from under the flap nearest you, holding the napkin firmly with the other hand.

5 Flatten the flap to make a point at each end, then swing the right-hand point down towards you; this forms two blades.

6 Turn the napkin round and repeat steps 4 and 5 to form the remaining two blades of the pinwheel.

The shirt

This is a clever design that is really much easier to make up than it looks. Make it with impeccably pressed and starched linen or cotton napkins, either plain or in smart stripes or checks.

1 Arrange the napkin right side down and fold all four corners to the centre.

2 Fold the two side edges of the square in to meet in the centre.

3 At the upper edge, fold a slender strip behind to form the collar.

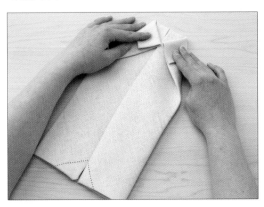

4 Fold the upper corners in so that they meet at the vertical centre line a short way from the top edge.

5 Fold out the right flap from the lower corner; the angle is not critical but the point should protrude beyond the outer edge.

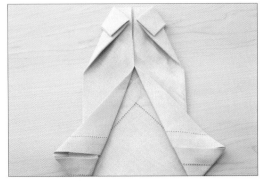

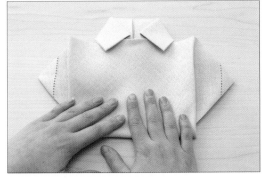

6 Fold out the left-hand flap from the same point on the vertical centre line. The points of these two flaps form the sleeves.

7 Fold up the lower edge and tuck it underneath the points of the collar created in step 4.

Bow tie

For a grand dinner at which the guests are formally dressed, you can match the bow ties of the men with this snappy design, which is suitable for napkins of a fairly modest size.

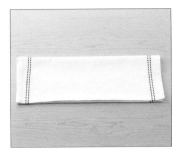

1 Open out the napkin with right side down and fold it horizontally into thirds, folding the upper portion down over the lower portion.

2 Fold the left-hand edge across to the right-hand edge.

3 At the left-hand, folded edge, fold in both corners at 45 degrees so that the edges meet horizontally in the centre.

4 Unfold the corners. Lift up the lower top layer and push the corner in between the layers along the creases made previously.

5 Flatten the napkin with the corner now turned inside. Repeat the process with the upper corner.

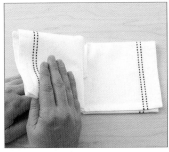

6 Lift up the top half of the napkin at the right-hand edge, and fold it back to the left as far as it will go: the crease will run along the edges of the small tucks.

7 Turn the napkin over and repeat step 6 on the reverse. At the folded edges, again fold in the outer corners at 45 degrees.

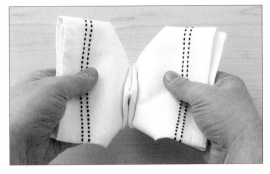

8 Carefully holding the edges and all the folds previously made at the centre, open out the two large flaps.

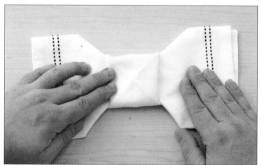

9 Allow the central point to flatten into a square; hold all the corner flaps firmly until this begins to happen.

10 Smooth out the central square and shape the napkin by folding the four outer corners back.

Papillon

The brighter and more varied the colours of the napkin you use for this design, the more glamorous will be the butterfly that emerges. Begin with the patterned side of the napkin face down.

1 Arrange the napkin in a square and fold the bottom edge up to the top.

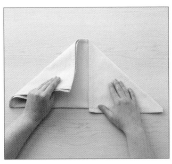

2 Fold both upper corners down at 45 degrees to lie along the centre line.

3 Turn the napkin over. Fold the right side in to lie along the centre line.

4 Fold in the left-hand side in the same way to meet the first side in the centre.

5 Slide out the loose corner from beneath each side, creating a diamond-shaped outline.

6 Turn the napkin over from side to side so the loose layers are underneath.

7 Fold down the top point and tuck it into the pocket formed by the horizontal edge.

8 Press the fold flat and arrange the butterfly on the plate or table.

9 To create the body, push the wings together to make a narrow pleat at the centre. The upper wing tips should move up slightly while the tips of the tail wings should spread apart a little.

Oriental fold

This eye-catching design with a Japanese feel requires two fabric napkins, which are folded together. One should be larger than the other and for the best effect they should be in contrasting colours.

1 Arrange the small napkin right side down and cover it with the larger napkin, also right side down, making sure the centre points match. Holding both napkins, fold all the corners into the centre.

2 Carefully turn the square over and fold up the bottom third, letting the loose corners straighten out.

3 Fold down the top third, again allowing the loose corners to open out.

4 At each end, tuck the top corners into the triangular flaps beneath them.

The place mat

If you have pretty plates you don't want to hide, or are planning to put the first course on the table before your guests sit down to eat, this fold enables you to arrange the napkins under the plates.

1 With the napkin right side up, fold in half bottom to top. Fold one layer of each upper corner down to the centre line.

2 Unfold the triangle by pulling the point toward you. Rotate the napkin 180 degrees and repeat step 1. Unfold to make a diamond.

3 Fold the four corners in to the centre, making sure the flaps underneath are not allowed to slide out of place.

4 Carefully holding all the flaps in place, turn the napkin over. Fold all the hemmed edges out diagonally from the centre to the corners.

Rose

This beautiful stylized rose, with its cleverly interwoven petals, will sit easily on plates of any size and can be folded successfully using either starched fabric or stiff paper napkins.

1 Arrange the open napkin right side down and fold all four corners to the centre.

2 Turn the napkin over and arrange as a diamond. Fold the lower right-hand sloping edge inward to lie along the horizontal diagonal.

3 Working anticlockwise, repeat step 2 with the next two edges, each overlapping its neighbour.

4 Fold in the final edge, but as you do so turn the flap in on itself and allow to tuck underneath.

5 The design should appear symmetrical. This concept is rather like locking together the four flaps of a cardboard box to keep it closed.

6 Lift up one of the loose corners and pull it across and over the edge of its anti-clockwise neighbour, allowing the pocket formed across the corner to flatten.

7 Once all the flaps have been folded across, this will cause the napkin to form an octagonal shape.

8 Tuck the four loose corners inside the four pockets created by flattening the folds in step 6.

9 Pull out the corners from beneath to suggest extra petals. This move will bring the overall shape back to a square once more.

10 Fold up the small corners at the centre of the rose to create the inner petals.

Pyramid

This spare geometric design makes an elegant treatment for beautiful napkins with an interesting texture or weave, and looks wonderful in a setting of streamlined, modern tableware.

1 Arrange the open napkin right side down and begin by folding all four corners to the centre.

2 Repeat the previous step with the new smaller square.

3 Fold all four corners in to meet at the centre point.

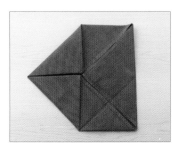

4 Rotate the napkin to form a diamond shape and open out the two right-hand corners.

5 Lift the upper section towards you, and as you do so make an inward fold in the right-hand side to take the top right corner to the bottom right corner.

6 Flatten the inner fold from the apex of the pyramid. You now have a double corner at the lower right-hand side.

7 Fold both layers of the corner as one inside on the existing crease, taking the points to the apex of the pyramid.

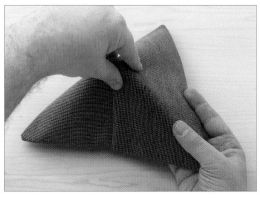

8 Turn the napkin over and carefully straighten all the folds before standing it on the table.

Pockets and parcels

Many popular napkin folds create flaps and pockets into which you can tuck anything from a place card to a bread roll. On a buffet table it's convenient to use folded napkins to keep sets of cutlery organized, while ingeniously folded napkins of every size can even conceal a surprise gift for each guest.

Buffet parcel

This practical idea keeps the cutlery tidy and, as it uses two napkins, provides an improvised tablemat as well as a napkin when opened. You will need two napkins of different colours.

1 Place the two napkins, right sides down, one on top of the other, staggered so that a strip of the lower one is visible at the top.

2 Fold the napkins in half vertically as one, then place the cutlery in the centre and fold the long sides over it.

3 ◁ Pick up the end nearest to you, and fold over about one third of the roll.

4 ▷ Fold the top end of the roll down and tuck it into the other end.

Picnic set

Use this simple, smart arrangement to keep sets of cutlery and napkins neatly together in a picnic basket or on a party table. You could use a length of ribbon or a raffia tie in place of the napkin ring.

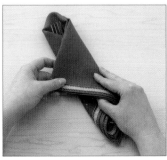

1 Fold the napkin into quarters. Place the knife and fork in the centre, arranging them diagonally.

2 Wrap the two sides of the napkin around the cutlery.

3 Slide a napkin ring over the bundle to hold the napkin and cutlery in place.

The cable

With its crisp diagonal folds, this rectangular napkin fold looks smart on any dinner table just as it is, but it also has the advantage of creating a pocket into which you can fit a set of cutlery.

1 Fold the napkin into quarters and arrange as a square with the open corners at top right.

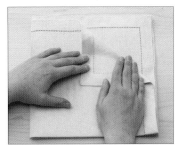

2 Pick up a single layer at the top right corner and fold it at 45 degrees so that the point is at the centre of the square.

3 Double the fold made in the previous step so that the diagonal folded edge lies over the point at the centre.

4 Making the fold on the central diagonal, double this layer over again.

5 Fold the top right corner of the next layer down to the bottom left corner.

6 Fold this layer back so that the point is touching the centre, as before.

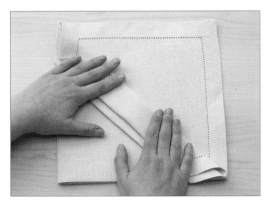

7 Double the fold made in the previous step so that the diagonal folded edge lies over the point at the centre, as in step 3.

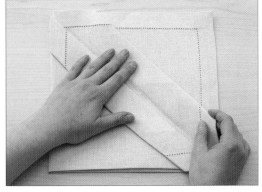

8 Double this layer over along the central diagonal. This creates two matching diagonal "stripes" across the napkin.

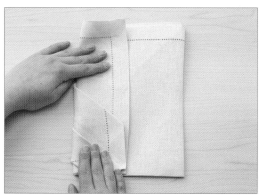

9 Turn the napkin over from side to side. The diagonal folds (now on the underside) run from bottom left to top right. Fold the left-hand vertical edge over to the left by a third.

10 Fold over the right-hand third and tuck the lower corner into the pocket created by the folds in the left-hand section. Turn the napkin over.

Envelope

Use this easy envelope fold to conceal a tiny gift or a few chocolate mints. It looks especially effective if you use napkins with a corner motif, which should be positioned on the right to begin the fold.

1 Arrange the open napkin, right side down, as a diamond. Fold it in half, taking the bottom corner up to the top, and fold in the left-hand side by a third.

2 Fold in the right-hand side so that the sharp point reaches the left-hand corner.

3 Open out the layers of the sharp point now at the bottom left corner and fold it back at the centre to form a small diamond.

4 Fold down the top corner and tuck it into the diamond at the bottom to close the envelope.

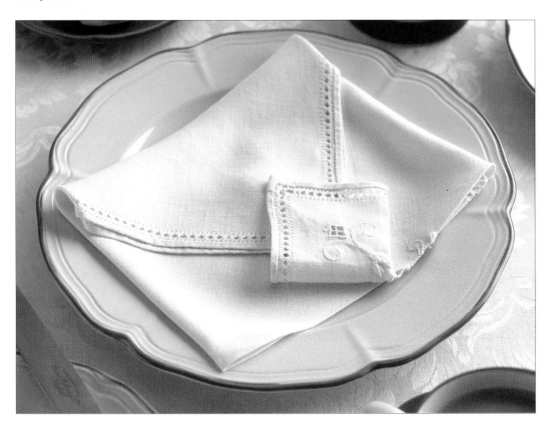

Decorative pocket

This clever design makes an attractive pocket in which to place anything from eating implements to a flower. It is another very effective way of displaying napkins with a corner motif.

1 Fold the napkin into quarters, wrong side out, and arrange as a diamond with the open corners at the top. If there is a corner motif, fold the napkin so that it is on the third layer down.

2 Fold down a single layer from the top, leaving a narrow border around the two lower sloping edges.

3 ◁ Fold down the next two layers in the same way, positioning each corner a little above the previous one.

4 ▷ Fold the side corners back, positioning the vertical creases so that they frame the corner motif, and open out the pouch to insert the cutlery.

Japanese pleats

The two rolled sections of this fold create a perfect support for a place card and a sprig of leaves or flowers, which soften the strict minimal look. Use a densely woven fabric that will hold the shape.

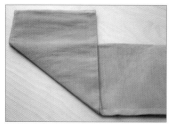

1 Fold the napkin into thirds to make a rectangular strip. Fold up the left side of the rectangle at 45 degrees so that the vertical folded edge aligns with the centre of the strip.

2 Fold up the right side of the napkin to match the left, then turn the napkin over so that the point is at the top. Roll up the lower flaps tightly until they meet the fold and hold in place with pins.

3 Turn the napkin over again so the point is at the bottom. Fold the left-hand triangle in half, bringing the roll down to the central fold. Repeat with the right-hand side, so that the two rolls lie together and the base is a square. Remove the pins and add a place card and flowers.

Cable buffet

In this compact design the folds of the napkin are securely locked together around the cutlery, allowing guests at a buffet or picnic to help themselves to napkin, knife and fork all at once.

1 Fold the bottom edge of the napkin up to the top, then fold the top of this layer down to the bottom fold.

2 Fold all the layers back up a little way at the bottom and turn the napkin over.

3 Fold the right-hand side of the napkin into the centre. Fold in the left-hand side so that the edges meet.

4 Fold the napkin vertically down the centre, tucking the bottom of one half into the folds on the other. Turn over.

Gift-wrapped

If you are presenting each of your guests with a gift at the table, this is a speedy and flamboyant way to wrap it up. Starch the napkins stiffly so that the corners stand up dramatically.

1 Open the napkin out flat, right side down, and centre the gift on it.

2 Gather the sides of the napkin around the gift, keeping the gathers even and holding all the edges in your hand.

3 Slide a napkin ring over the edges and push it down over the gift to keep the package taut. Adjust the gathers.

Parcelled surprise

This is a neat way to conceal a gift in a square or rectangular box, to give guests a surprise as they open their napkins on celebration days such as Christmas or Easter, or even at a wedding.

1 Arrange the open napkin right side down and position the box diagonally in the centre. Lift two opposite points of the napkin and hold them together.

2 Fold the points over and over again, together, until the fold lies neatly on top of the box.

3 ◁ Fold in the excess fabric at either side of the box and press flat to form a narrow strip.

4 ▷ Pull the ends of the strips up together and knot them on top of the box to secure the parcel.

Waiter's jacket

This classic design is ideal for more formal dinners, where it can be used to display a menu card, but it requires practice to get the proportions right. You will need large, starched cotton napkins.

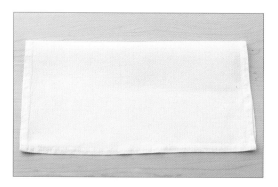

1 Arrange the napkin as a square and fold it in half, taking the top edge down to the bottom.

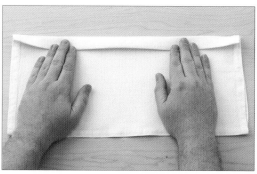

2 Turn over a narrow fold at the top folded edge, to create the collar. Press in position.

3 Turn the napkin over from side to side. Fold down the left-hand side at an angle a short way from the centre.

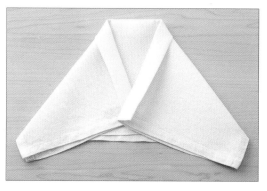

4 Fold down the right side to match, so that the two flaps overlap slightly at the lower edge.

5 Shape the left side of the jacket by folding the edge of the napkin back at the desired angle.

6 Fold back the right side to match, holding the lapels in place at the front.

7 Fold the lower edge underneath to neaten the design. (If you are inserting a card in the napkin, do this first.)

Place card holder

This flat fold makes a compact shape that sits discreetly on the table or on a small plate, and is just the right size to display a place card. It can be made with either fabric or paper napkins.

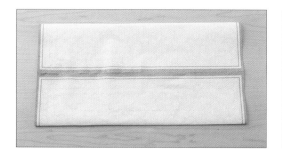

1 With the open napkin right side down, fold the upper and lower edges into the centre.

2 Fold all four corners at 45 degrees, so that the edges lie along the horizontal centre line.

3 Fold the left-hand side across to the right, making the crease a little further in than the ends of the corner folds.

4 Fold the right-hand side over in the same way, so that there is a symmetrical triangular notch at top and bottom.

5 Turn the napkin over from side to side. Fold the lower edge up by a third, and fold the upper edge down to match.

6 Tuck the two corners of the top flap into the diagonal pockets of the lower portion to hold the folds in place. Finally, tuck the place card inside the diagonal pockets.

Salt cellar

The salt cellar is a well-known traditional origami design: children often use it to tell fortunes, writing a message under each flap. Made with a beautifully starched napkin you can use it to hold nibbles.

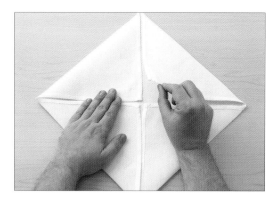

1 Arrange the open napkin right side down and fold all four corners into the centre.

2 Holding the folds in place, turn the napkin over and again fold all four of the new outer corners into the centre.

3 Rotate the napkin so that it is square, and fold it in half from bottom to top.

4 Holding each half of the rectangle between your fingers and thumbs, push the ends in, allowing the sides to collapse outwards; as your fingers and thumbs come together all four outer corners will meet at the bottom.

5 Hold the napkin together at the bottom and carefully tease open the corners at the top to create four pockets.

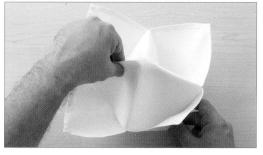

6 Adjust the folds and the shape of the pockets so that the design will stand securely.

Bread basket

Large napkins can be turned into attractive containers. Fold your guests' napkins in this way to hold a bread roll at each place setting, or use a few of these "baskets" to serve crackers or breadsticks.

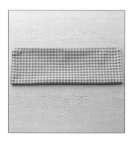

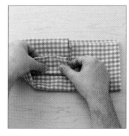
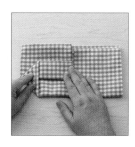

1 With the napkin arranged as a square, right side down, fold it into thirds, folding the bottom third over the top third.

2 Fold the left-hand edge of the rectangle over toward the right by one third.

3 Fold the lower side edge of this flap over, again by one third of the width of the flap. At the folded end of the section the corner rises and does not lie flat.

4 Allow the end of the fold to flatten into a small triangle at the lower left-hand corner of the napkin.

5 Fold the upper third of the left-hand flap down over the previous fold, again flattening the end into a triangle.

6 Fold the narrow strip in the centre out to the left over the triangles.

7 Repeat steps 2 to 6 on the right-hand side of the napkin. The design should now appear symmetrical.

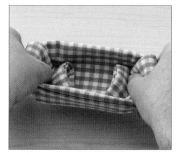

8 Place your thumbs inside the basket and open it out while holding the flaps at the ends in place with your fingers.

9 Turn the basket over, placing your fingers inside with your thumbs holding the strips in place on the outside.

10 Turn the basket inside out, pushing the flaps down inside and bringing the sides up with your fingers.

Sampan

This useful design makes an elegantly slim container for crackers or fruit. Use a densely woven napkin that will hold the creases well. The length of the finished sampan is the width of the napkin.

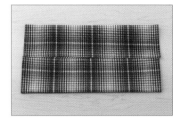

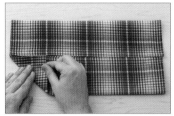

1 Arrange the napkin right side down in a square and fold the upper and lower edges to the centre.

2 Fold a corner of the rectangle in at 45 degrees so that its edge lies along the horizontal centre line.

3 Repeat with the three other corners to create a lozenge shape.

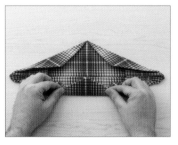

4 Double over the sloping edges so that they meet at the centre line. The folds should start at the centre of the napkin on each side.

5 Fold the lower point to the centre and repeat with the upper point.

6 Holding the napkin between fingers and thumbs as shown, open out the innermost flaps, and grasp these firmly along with the flaps folded in step 5.

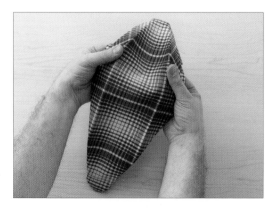

7 Carefully turn the napkin over, still holding the sides and inner flaps in place. With your thumbs, push down carefully on each of the shallow outer corners, at the same time turning the sides inside out to lock the sampan into shape.

8 Turn the sampan round and shape the other end in the same way. Flatten the base and shape the sides so that it is stable.

Templates

Trace the templates and enlarge them to the desired size. Cut out the tracing and draw around it on to thin cardboard. Cut out carefully and accurately to create a template. When drawing around a template on to fabric use a water- or air-soluble marker pen.

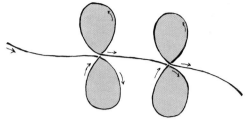

Above *Couched organza p58*

Above *Fretwork-style felt p84*

Above *Hand-painted motif p67*

Above *Cupid p59*

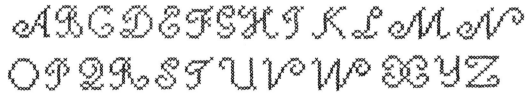

Above *Painted "cross stitch" napkin p69*

Above *Painted "cross-stitch" napkin p69*

Above *Lemon slice napkin p61*

Above *Cross-stitch heart p64*
**Punched metal napkin ring p88*

a b c d e e f ç h i j k l m
n o p q r s t u v w x y z

Above *Monograms p63*

Stitches

The stitches illustrated below are all used in the projects within the Making and Decorating Napkins For All Occasions chapter.

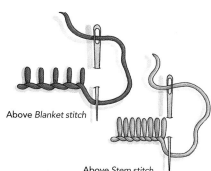

Above *Blanket stitch*

Above *Stem stitch*

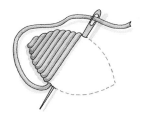

Above *Satin stitch*

Above *Chain stitch*

Above *Running stitch*

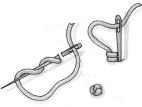

Above *French knot*

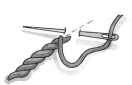

Above *Stem stitch*

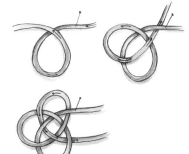

Above *Cross stitch*

Above *Fly stitch*

Above *Couching*

Above *Turk's head knot*

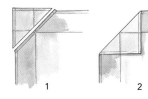

Above *Mitring a corner*

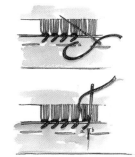

Above *Drawn-thread work*

Above *Slip stitch*

Index

This edition is published by Southwater, an imprint of Anness Publishing Ltd, Blaby Road, Wigston, Leicestershire LE18 4SE; info@anness.com

www.southwaterbooks.com; www.annesspublishing.com

If you like the images in this book and would like to investigate using them for publishing, promotions or advertising, please visit our website www.practicalpictures.com for more information.

© Anness Publishing Ltd 2012

A CIP catalogue record for this book is available from the British Library.

Publisher: **Joanna Lorenz**
Editorial Director: **Helen Sudell**
Editor: **Simona Hill**
Designer: **Lisa Tai**
Production Controller: **Wendy Lawson**
Photography and Styling:
All photography by **Mark Wood** and styling by **Helen Trent** except for the following: **Spike Powell** and **Andrea Spencer** 4tl, 4tr, 4trc, 5tl, 7l, 10–11, 12, 20–21, 22, 23, 24, 25, 26, 27, 28, 29, 30tr, 31bl, 32bl, 32tr, 32br, 34l, 35bl, 35tr, 37, 38, 39tr, 40, 41bl, 44, 45, 46, 47, 48–9, 50, 51, 54, 55, 56, 58, 65, 67, 70–71, 72, 73, 77, 78b, 79, 80, 81b, 82b, 83, 84, 86b, 87, 89r, 92–93, 94, 95, 110, 112t, 113b, 119t, 123t, 124l, 125tr, 126, 137tr, 147, 153, 163, 203tl, 203tr, 205, 209t, 211t, 231tr, 231tl, 235t, 238t, 241. **Nicki Dowey** 42bl, 43bl (maker **Susie Stokoe**). **Paul Bricknell** 53. **Debbie Patterson** and **Tessa Evelegh** 5, 18, 19, 33tl, 35br, 41, 75. **Michelle Garrett** 13b, 61 (maker **Dorothy Wood**), 69, with **Tessa Evelegh** 76, with **Gilly Love** 34tr, 34br, with **Alison Jenkins** 45, and **Karin Hossack** 69, with **Stewart** and **Sally Walton** 43tr and 68. **Polly Wreford** and **Tessa Evelegh** 16, 17, 36, 39bl, 39br, 42tl, 43tc, 57, 59, 62, 64t, 64b, 74, 85, 88. **Steve Wooster** 6. **Caroline Arber** and **Charlotte Melling** 15. **Frank Adam** and **Craig Robertson** 30tl, 30bl, 30br.

NOTES

NOTES

NOTES

NOTES

NOTES

NOTES

NOTES

NOTES